061/498-70
TAXI

CW01025139

Publisher
buybook
Radićeva 4, Sarajevo
Telephone: +387 33 716-450, 716-451
Zelenih beretki 8, Sarajevo
+387 33 712-010, 712-011
E-mail: fabrikaknjiga@buybook.ba
www.buybook.ba

For Publisher
Goran Samardžić
Damir Uzunović

Authors
Tim Clancy
Willem van Eekelen

Contributing author
John Snyder

Design
Nedim Meco

Printed in Croatia by Zrinski

CIP - Katalogizacija u publikaciji
Nacionalna i univerzitetska biblioteka
Bosne i Hercegovine, Sarajevo

338.483 (497.6) (036)

CLANCY, Tim
    Sarajevo : a guided journey through Sarajevo
and the surrounding areas / Tim Clancy, Willem van
Eekelen. - Sarajevo : Buybook, 2005. - 163 str. :
ilustr. ; 22 cm

ISBN 9958-630-60-5
1. Eekelen, Willem van
COBISS.BH-ID 13953286

A GUIDED JOURNEY THROUGH

SARAJEVO

AND THE SURROUNDING AREAS

Tim Clancy
Willem van Eekelen

buybook

Sarajevo, 2005

A guide to Sarajevo

It is true that the city of Sarajevo has been a
dear friend of mine, but so much of its meaning to me
comes through you Sabina.

Ti si meni sve naj, naj.

THE SERIES

As Bosnia and Herzegovina emerges as one of the newest and most exciting tourist destinations in Europe, there is a growing need for detailed and thorough information on this country. In response to this demand **buybook** publishing company now offers a series of new books that cover the cultural, historical, natural and culinary heritage of Bosnia and Herzegovina. Four books are on the shelves already:

- Sarajevo and the surrounding areas
- Herzegovina
- Central and North Bosnia
- Forgotten Beauty – Hiking to BiH's highest peaks

More titles are to follow.

The first part of the regional guides is a general introduction to Bosnia and Herzegovina. This section is the same for each of the guides and provides you with the standard information needed to enjoy a journey in any part of the country. The second part of each guide is a comprehensive and region-specific travel companion, covering hotels, restaurants, café's and clubs, transport, travel agencies and a wide range of activities for all types of visitor. Each guide also has an eco-tourism section highlighting the natural beauties, flora and fauna, wildlife photography, fly-fishing, and more. The guides cover all major destinations, but also a great many places that are off the beaten track. In many cases, you will need a detailed map to find these hidden treasures.

Welcome to the brighter side of Bosnia and Herzegovina – enjoy your trip!!

CONTENTS

ACKNOWLEDGEMENTS

We're happy to say that there are many people to thank. Where to start? Let's go full circle... this project started in 2001, during our hike in one of Europe's last primeval forests in Sutjeska National Park. Two things struck us: this was the most beautiful place we had ever seen, and there wasn't a soul in sight. Tourists, apparently, didn't know about this country's beauty.

Three years later, in the spring of 2004, Paddy Ashdown and three representatives from Bosnia and Herzegovina traveled around Europe to shed some light on this hidden little treasure called Bosnia and Herzegovina. This generated, perhaps for the first time, large scale interest in the 'lighter side' of this country. To turn interest into visits, people need information – henceforth, our chance to write this booklet!

The creation of this series had many contributors. The Japan International Cooperation Agency allowed us to use their wonderful research, which greatly enhanced the eco-tourism section of this series. John Snyder did some of the best research on wildlife habitats, fly-fishing, fish species identification and the entire eco-tourism package to date. The European Youth Group, with its great corps of volunteers, did great research on Sarajevo and Banja Luka. Boris Rebac, Barbara-Anne Krijgsman and many people at the various tourism associations suggested valuable additions. Jim Marshall did many fine-tunings to the text and his tremendous knowledge of the conflict will certainly help the reader understand a bit better what happened here. Others wrote texts as well – as is indicated in the text. Thanks to Trudi Bolten and Hans van Eekelen too: they edited the first part of this booklet.

Azra Skajlo at Green Visions showed once again how patient she can be after we repeatedly placed tasks on her desk to check and double-check phone numbers, addresses and whatever else was needed. Thanks Azra. The same thanks go to Suad Salkić, who spent many evenings verifying and adding all sorts of things.

Brank Media were very generous and allowed us to use some of their amazing photographs. The Dutch Embassy kindly covered much of the costs of producing this series. For that to happen, Hans de Vries did his bit of proposal writing – and came to love the country so much that he is now married to Sabina. Thanks Hans, and congratulations!

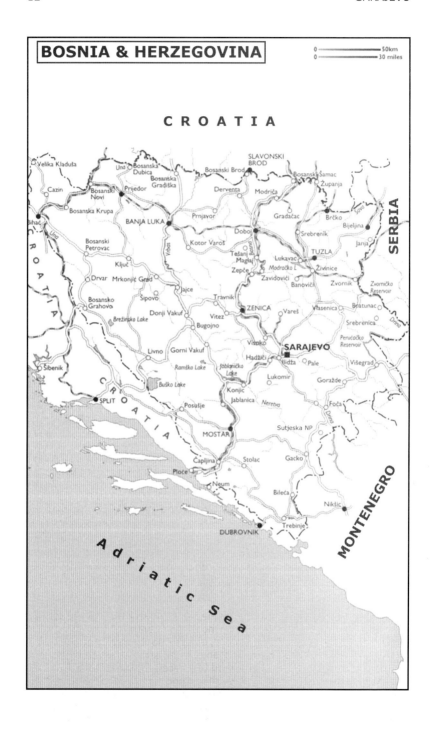

Part one: THE COUNTRY

BACKGROUND INFORMATION

Facts & Figures

Location: Southeast Europe, bordering Croatia (932 km), Serbia (312 km) and Montenegro (215 km)

Land area: 51,129 km^2

Status: Republic

Languages: Bosnian, Croatian, Serbian

Population: probably around 3.8 million

Religions: Muslim (44%), Orthodox Christian (32%), Roman Christian (17%), Others (7%)

Capital: Sarajevo, with a population of around 400,000

Other major cities and towns in the country: Banja Luka, Tuzla, Zenica, Mostar, Bihać

Administrative division: The country is divided into two entities: the Federation of Bosnia and Herzegovina, and the Republika Srpska. The Federation of Bosnia and Herzegovina is subdivided into ten cantons.

Time: CET (GMT + 1 hour)

Currency: Convertible Mark (KM or BAM)

International telephone code: +387

Bosnia and Herzegovina is a long name for a country that measures just over 50,000 km^2. Bosnia covers the north and centre of the country. Its name is probably derived from 'bosana', an old Indo-European word meaning water, and refers to the country's many rivers, streams and springs. The southern region of ancient Hum, ruled by Herceg Stjepan (Duke Stjepan), was later named Herzegovina after the region was conquered by the invading Ottomans. Together, these two areas form a triangular country in the middle of what used to be Yugoslavia. It is a mountainous country that borders on Croatia and Serbia & Montenegro, two other former Yugoslav republics. It is here that eastern and western civilizations met, often clashed but also enriched and reinforced each other.

GEOGRAPHY

The trip from Sarajevo to Mostar is a two-hour drive. Halfway, a tunnel links Bosnia to Herzegovina. On the one side of this tunnel there is lush vegetation on gently rolling hills. On the other side there are the high, rugged mountains of the Dinaric Alps. This mountain range is the natural boundary of the Mediterranean and continental Alpine climates. The warm Adriatic temperatures clash with the harsher Alpine ones, producing one of the most diverse eco-systems in Europe. A bit further towards Mostar, these mountains are gone again and you are in a fertile flatland. That is Bosnia and Herzegovina: three worlds in a two hour drive. Had I been in a different bus when writing this section, I would have started it with moonlands, waterfalls, piping hot spring water steaming up to the road, snow (in May), fierce rivers, thick medieval forests and green mountain lakes.

Land

Much of Bosnia and Herzegovina is mountainous. The long chain of the Southern Alps – the Dinaric Alps - stretches from northwest Croatia through the heart of Bosnia and Herzegovina and into Montenegro, and finishes in the Prokletija Mountains on the Albanian border. Herzegovina hosts the highest and wildest of this mountain range, which for centuries provided the population protection from Roman invaders, and which slowed the Ottoman conquest of Bosnia.

Other parts of the country – even the other mountainous parts - look very different from the rugged Alpines. The central belt of Bosnia has both rocky mountains and green, rolling hills covered with conifer forests and lined with countless freshwater streams and rivers. Some northern areas are part of the long and agriculturally rich plains that extend from Hungary, through Slavonia and Croatia into the fertile fields of the Sava and Drina River valleys. Part of the northwest of the country is all karst topography, with deep limestone caves and underground rivers. These limestone fields are connected to the low limestone valleys of the south. Together, they form the single largest karst field in the world.

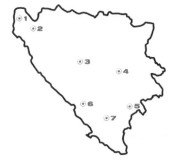

Waterfalls

1. Bukovi na Uni ili Veliki slap
2. Štrbački buk
3. Vodopad Plive
4. Vodopad Skakavac
5. Vodopad Skakavci
6. Kravice
7. Provalija

Mountains

1. Maglić, 2396m
2. Volujak, 2336m
3. Velika Ljubušnja, 2238m
4. Čvrsnica, 2226m
5. Vranica, 2110m
6. Prenj, 2103m
7. Treskavica, 2086m
8. Vran, 2074m
9. Bjelašnica, 2067m
10. Lelija, 2032m
11. Zelengora,2014m
12. Cincar, 2006m

Mountains in Bosnia and Herzegovina

The Dinaric mountains

From the high central ranges, the Dinaric Alps cut east towards Visočica, Bjelašnica, and Treskavica Mountains. This area has some very deep canyons. Many of the highland settlements here date back to medieval times. Moving further east, bordering Montenegro, are Bosnia and Herzegovina's highest peaks. Protected in Sutjeska National Park, Maglić Mountain (2,386m) towers above the surrounding natural fortresses of Zelengora Mountain, Volujak, Lelija and the Mesozoic walls of Lebršnik Mountain. The young limestone mountains of the Dinaric system can be found in the middle part of the county. Together, these three sub-areas are good for ten peaks above the 2000 metre mark.

Vran	2074m
Čvrsnica	2226m
Čabulja	1789m
Velež	1969m
Prenj	2103m
Bjelašnica	2067m
Visočica	1974m
Crvanj	1921m
Treskavica	2086m
Lelija	2032m
Zelengora	2014m
Ljubišna	2242m
Volujak	2336m
Maglić	2396m (highest peak in the country)

Then, there is the mountain range that forms the natural connection between Herzegovina and Bosnia.

Ivan	950m
Makljen	1123m
Kupreška vrata	1324m
Čemerno	1293m

And lastly, to the north, next to the river Sava and the low basin of the Bosna River, lies the flat valley of Posavina, surrounded by a long stretch of low mountains. These mountains are not high, but they are impressive as they rise like lonely islands out of the valley.

Majevica	916m
Motajnica	652m
Vučjak	368m
Prosara	363m
Kozara	977m

Water

Bosnia and Herzegovina is a country full of water. Much of that water flows under the ground. You can hear it, but you can't always see it. Some underground water exits in the form of submarine springs in the Adriatic Sea. Other water gushes from mountain sides, in springs that come hot and cold and in all shapes and intensities. Many springs appear as a gentle stream, but in Blagaj it's a whole river that gushes out of the mountain. Most water is crystal clear, but some water carries such a density of minerals that the water is colored.

Some water feeds into lakes. The Deransko-Svitavsko Lakes are part of Hutovo blato, a large bird reserve in the south of the country. Boračko Lake and Blidinje Lake are equally beautiful and maintain their own eco-systems. Perhaps even more spectacular are the glacial lakes in the mountain regions of Prenj, Čvrsnica, Satora, Vranica, Treskavica, Crvanj and Volujak.

The country's biggest lake - Buško Lake – is manmade. With an average size of 55km^2, this lake was formed by regulating the waters of the Livanjsko and Duvanjsko valleys, destroying, as artificial lakes often do, unique eco-systems in the process. The most popular tourist lakes are artificial as well: the lakes of Jablanica and Modrac, both formed by hydro-electric dams.

CLIMATE

In Bosnia and Herzegovina, Mediterranean and Alpine influences meet and create a mosaic of climate types within a relatively small area. The south enjoys warm, sunny and dry weather, with very mild winters. In the more continental areas the weather is similar to that of central Europe – hot summers, cool springs and autumns, and cold winters with considerable snowfall. The Mediterranean and continental climates meet in the middle, creating eco-systems that cannot be found anywhere else.

The mountains create a climate of their own. The Alpine climate rules the mountain terrains of the high Dinarics above 1700 meters. The winters there are extremely cold, with temperatures well below zero for more than six months of the year. Snow covers the terrain until summer and the winds often reach hurricane strength.

FLORA AND FAUNA

Bosnia and Herzegovina faces the challenge of preserving its natural wealth, and it is not well prepared. Less than one percent of Bosnia and Herzegovina's land surface is protected – compared to the European average of seven percent – and the country risks losing much of its pristine wilderness and forests to uncontrolled development, clear cutting, and exploitation of its abundant fresh water supply.

Flora

Beech, oak, evergreen, chestnut, spruce and dozens of other types of trees form thick forests that cover over a third of the country. Conversely, black pines often stand alone. Shaped like skinny mushrooms, they do not require earth and grow on rocks, sometimes all alone on otherwise barren mountainsides.

Many of the country's forests are absolutely spectacular, but none matches the rough beauty of Perućica forest. This primeval forest dates back over 20,000 years. It lays in a valley, hidden below Maglić Mountain, the country's highest peak. Here, massive beech trees are complemented by the high black pines that grow on the rock faces that surround the valley. A hike through the heart of these woodlands is an unforgettable and awe-inspiring experience.

The climates suit a surprising variety of plants and trees. The country's central and eastern forests are very similar to those found in northern and central Europe. Herzegovina and western Bosnia, which are covered by large areas of karst, are characterized by vegetation typical of the coastal and mountainous regions of the Mediterranean.

Unsurprisingly, the country's two large floral regions intersect along the same lines, and have a richness that only tropical and sub-tropical regions can match. Very favorable conditions have preserved species from the times of diluvia glaciations right up to the present. Together, the Euro-Siberian and Mediterranean floral regions are home to over 3,700 species of flowering plants, including hundreds of endemic species (species that are unique to the region). If you like flowers, come in spring. You will see them, in their thousands, in all shapes, sizes and colors, and absolutely everywhere.

Fauna

Bosnia and Herzegovina was once home to one of the largest bear populations in the world and had thriving wolf, deer, wild boar and wild goat
communities. These populations suffered severely from the war. Throughout the conflict many frontlines were in the high mountain regions. This
exposed bear, wild goat, wild boar and wolf populations to heavy gun and
artillery fire, and to being hunted for food by soldiers. Many have been
killed, or fled to quieter forests in neighboring countries.

Despite their diminished numbers it is not uncommon to see a bear,
or occasionally a wolf, in Sutjeska National Park in eastern Bosnia. Most
wild goats live in Herzegovina's Neretva Valley, but some are found in
Sutjeska National Park and on the southern slopes of Bjelašnica and Visočica
Mountains as well. Wild boars have even made a real comeback and are
experiencing population overgrowth. They are usually found in lush, conifer areas in the medium sized mountain ranges but can be occasionally be
spotted in Herzegovina as well. In addition, there are foxes, otters, pine
martens, bobcats, deer, porcupines, many types of snakes and a variety of
other little creatures in the country's large stretches of untouched wilderness.

There is a plethora of birds as well. Hutovo blato is the largest bird
migration centre in southeast Europe. In these marshy wetlands in southern Herzegovina you can find 240 types of birds, many of them on a migration path between Europe and North Africa. Heron, Greek partridge, coot,
owls, pheasants, and wild duck permanently make their home in this tiny
oasis. The Brdača Reserve in the north of the country is also a haven for
many types of birds and is in the process of attaining protection status. But
you don't have to come to parks to see rare birds. The high mountains
have always been home to eagles, hawks and falcons and it is not uncommon to see them on a walk or hike almost anywhere in the country. Driving
on the main highway from Bihać towards Bosanski Petrovac you are almost
guaranteed to spot large hawks perched on the old electricity cables lining
the road.

Illegal hunting

In talks about the tourism potential of Bosnia and Herzegovina,
people in the business regularly list their hunting grounds as
attraction number one. Hunters should come to Bosnia and
Herzegovina, they say, and shoot bear. This is illegal, but apparently hunting regulation is so poorly enforced that some people
feel they can ignore it completely. That is most unfortunate, as
bear and other populations have been depleted as a consequence
of illegal hunting, mines, and a mass exodus during the war years.

Fish are abundant in Bosnia and Herzegovina. Most of the fresh water
rivers are teeming with trout. Carp, grayling, and bass are found throughout the country. These fish are of some economic importance: the first
organized tour group that returned to Bosnia and Herzegovina after the
war was here for fly-fishing, and this type of tourism is bound to increase,
creating employment in otherwise rather peripheral parts of the country.

BOSNIA ENTITIES

CROATIA

KEY
- Entity boundary
- Cantonal boundary
- Country boundary
- Federation area
- Brčko District

POSAVINA CANTON

SERBIA

Prijedor

Bihać

UNA-SANA CANTON

BANJA LUKA

REPUBLIKA SRPSKA

Doboj

Brčko District

Brčko

Bijeljina

TUZLA CANTON

TUZLA

ZENICA-DOBOJ

Travnik

ZENICA CANTON

CENTRAL BOSNIA CANTON

REPUBLIKA SRPSKA

LIVNO CANTON

Livno

SARAJEVO CANTON

SARAJEVO

PODRINA CANTON

Goražde

HERCEGOVINA-NERETVA CANTON

WEST HERCEGOVINA CANTON

Foča

MOSTAR

REPUBLIKA SRPSKA

MONTENEGRO

Adriatic Sea

Nikšić

Trebinje

0 — 50km
0 — 30 miles

PEOPLE

The geography and climate of Bosnia and Herzegovina have had a profound influence on the country's people. A rugged and creative mountain
culture has emerged from this region, connecting man and nature in ways
rarely seen in modern times. Every second mountain walk will pass by an
ancient village that preserves 'old world' Europe. Here, modern medicines
and exotic spices will never replace the medicinal herbs that have long
been used to cure illnesses, heal wounds, improve circulation and spice up
meals.

In the open valleys between these mountains sprawl Mostar, Jablanica,
Konjic, Sarajevo, Foča and many other towns. They are all very old. Some
of them – Mostar, Travnik – once grew at strategic places along trade
routes. Others – Srebrenica, Tuzla – were founded on the wealth of minerals. Gold, silver, salt, and copper have all been mined here since Roman
times.

In the south, the rivers and Mediterranean climate offer ideal conditions for agricultural settlements, and the Neretva River Valley and the
Neretva Delta have been inhabited since the Paleolithic Age. These areas
produce fruits such as figs, oranges, mandarins, and pomegranates, and
have had a winemaking tradition since Roman times. In the north, water
has been equally valuable. Jointly, the Una, Sana and Vrbas Rivers have
long protected the area against invaders. The fertile valleys these rivers
created are sacred to their inhabitants, and guests will find these rivers
spoken of as members of the family.

DEMOGRAPHICS

According to the last population census there were 4,354,911 inhabitants
in Bosnia and Herzegovina in 1991. Due to war-related death and migration, that number is lower now. Policy makers estimate that the country's
population is now around 3.8 million people and steadily growing, and that
over one million Bosnians now live abroad. The ethnic composition remains
similar to the pre-war percentages: Bosniacs (Muslims) 44%, Serbs (Christian Orthodox) 32%, and Croats (Catholics) 17%. The remaining 7% of the
population is composed of Yugoslavs, Albanians, Gypsies, Jews, and several other minority groups.

If ever a new census were to be held, I would be intrigued to know the
population's division by sex. Wherever I look, I see more women than
men. Is that true, or could it be my flawed perspective? The war probably
had its impact. But isn't the male-dominated fighting compensated by the
female-dominated outward migration? I don't know. A few friends told me
that women have always outnumbered men in some of the country's main
towns and cities.

LANGUAGE

The politics of language

Americans speak English; Austrians speak German; and until not long ago the southern Slavs spoke Serbo-Croatian. The political fractions that occurred in the early 1990's brought along with it the politics of language as well. Bosnian, Croatian and Serbian barely differ at all, but are nonetheless considered three different languages. It is a political choice, not a linguistic reality, as the border police illustrated when I said the exact same sentence four times when driving from Sarajevo to Belgrade via Croatia:

Exiting Bosnia and Herzegovina: 'Hey, where did you learn to speak Bosnian?'

Entering Croatia: 'Hey, where did you learn to speak Croatian?'

Exiting Croatia: 'Hey, where did you learn to speak Croatian?'

Entering Serbia and Montenegro: 'Hey, where did you learn to speak Serbian?'

The pre-war language of former Yugoslavia was Serbo-Croat. This term is virtually extinct now. Nowadays, there are three 'official' languages spoken in Bosnia and Herzegovina: Bosnian, Croatian, and Serbian. Local people attach great importance to the name of the language. For practical purposes, these languages are one and the same. The differences are similar to those between American and British English.

Bosnian/Croatian/Serbian is a Slavic language. Many words are similar in Czech or Slovakian, even Polish and Ukrainian. The language is distinctly different from but part of the same family as Russian. Illustrating the common Ottoman past, there are many Ottoman words that Bosnia and Herzegovina shares with the Egyptian dialect of Arabic.

In the Federation only the Latin alphabet is used, but in the Republika Srpska, the other of the two entities of Bosnia and Herzegovina, many signs are in Cyrillic. This includes road signs. If you are unable to decipher that script you might find it difficult to know exactly where you are.

In the cities it is not uncommon to find English-speaking people. Because of the large refugee and migrant population that lived in Germany during the war there are many German speakers as well. In the rural areas neither language is spoken among the adults, but there may well be children able to chat with you in English. Some useful words and phrases can be found in the language section of the Appendix.

Sign Language

Although isolated by a large mountain range, Bosnia and Herzegovina possesses many Mediterranean characteristics. Body and hand language is one of them. If a non-English speaking person is having trouble communicating with you, be prepared for him or her using other means to get the message across. People here don't behave like British or Americans and just speak louder – they *move*. So:

- If a Bosnian makes a waving motion (sort of like 'come here') in the vicinity of his or her mouth: would you like to eat?
- If a local takes a hitchhiker's thumb and bobs it towards his or her mouth: would you like a drink?
- If one pinches the forefinger and thumb together, with the pinky finger out and gently bobs the hand: let's go for a coffee.
- If the right arm shoots up above the shoulder: either 'forget it' or 'screw you'...your call.
- If the right arm sweeps across the front of the chest like hitting a ball or something: 'don't worry about it'...'so what'
- A thumbs up does not mean you are great or that things are OK – it means one, the number one.
- The neck disappearing into the shoulders and both hands shrugging in front means 'it wasn't me' or 'how do I know?'
- The index and pointer finger, tapped against the lips: can you spare a cigarette?

ECONOMY

Imagine this. There is a place that goes through a devastating war. Before the war, the place was a relatively poor and underdeveloped part of a country with a centrally planned economy. After the war, the place is an independent nation in the midst of an intensely competitive free market world economy. Before the war, there used to be import protection and there were secure trade links with the wealthier republics of the country it then belonged to. In times of hardship, these wealthier republics cushioned the blows by providing some economic support. After the war, this now independent nation is bound by free trade agreements with the rest of the world. Even without any further impediments, businesses would find it almost impossible to compete successfully in this whole new setting. This place, obviously, is Bosnia and Herzegovina, and unfortunately there *are* further impediments.

Before the war, Bosnia and Herzegovina concentrated on the production of basic goods (wood, agricultural produce, iron bars) and intermediate products (parts of cars, parts of shoes, parts of furniture). Other regions of former Yugoslavia bought these intermediate products and used them to make final consumer products. Because of the war, these buyers had to find new suppliers. After the war, these buyers will only come back to their pre-war suppliers if these suppliers offer the best and cheapest products available on the world market. With factories in shambles, infrastructure destroyed and workers displaced or killed, producing the best and cheapest products is not an easy task.

The war came to an end with a peace agreement that dictates a horrifyingly complex government structure. A company has to deal with several layers of government, each of which has complicated and sometimes non-sensible legislation. A simple change of business address, for example, requires procedures at the level of the municipality, canton, entity, and state. New companies face complex pre-war anti-private sector legislation and a government that provides problems rather than support in return for tax money. The only companies that benefit from the government – in the form of subsidies – are the public companies of the past. Without government support, very few of them would stay in business. In many cases, they have become uncompetitive dinosaurs, using outdated equipment and led by people chosen for their political affiliation rather than their technical expertise.

Imagine all this. It is a miracle that Bosnia and Herzegovina has some sort of functioning economy at all.

Ever since the Dayton Peace Accords were signed at the end of 1995, Bosnia and Herzegovina has been in a long, slow and painful process of economic recovery. The reform process has been slow for a number of reasons. First, there is no tested recipe for the economic revitalisation of a place that left the world economy as part of a centrally planned country and re-emerged as a war-torn independent country in a competitive free-market economy. It is simply not known what such a country should do to adapt. Second, pro-business legislation causes harm in the short run. People will lose their jobs and this is a particularly bad time to lose one's job. For obvious reasons, politicians and people will resist such legislation. Third, the focus in the immediate post-war years has been on political consolidation, not economic development. Fourth, there are very few seasoned economists available. Even the international organizations often resort to recruiting junior anthropologists to tackle issues that require senior and specialized economists. And lastly: corrupt government officials and a thriving mafia have not been helpful.

And yet, not all is bad. The currency is strong, inflation is low, the country is not heavily indebted, and much of the infrastructure has by now been reconstructed. In addition, some bad indicators do not reflect reality. At roughly 40 percent, the official unemployment rate indicates a non-functioning economy. In reality, many people registered as unemployed work in the informal sector. Similarly, the people who moved abroad have proven to be exceptionally loyal to the people they left behind. In all likelihood, they will continue to send money in the years to come. Most economists do not consider remittances a healthy economic foundation and point out that these remittances allow for the continuation of an import-based economy. True, but there is a difference between the long-term perspective and the short-term needs: the fact is that, as in other unstable (post) war parts of the world – Lebanon, the Palestinian Territories - this cash inflow does keep things afloat in times of hardship.

The next few years will be crucial. Will Bosnia and Herzegovina be able to come closer to Europe? Will the country manage to cut back its bureaucracy, privatise its public companies, and attract investments? Will logging, agriculture, steel, mining, services, textiles and building materials be the economic pillars of the future, or will new sectors arise? Will the country manage to utilise more fully its potential in agriculture (with a competitive advantage in organic farming), eco-tourism, hydro-electric power (many large dams function at only a quarter of their full potential), and wood-processing? Will the country perhaps regain its role as a producer of intermediate goods, once again supplying factories in the surrounding countries? When I look at many of the politicians, I am not very hopeful. But when I visit trade fairs and see an ever-increasing number of young companies that successfully identified market niches, I tend to think that Bosnia and Herzegovina has a bright future to look forward to.

RELIGION

In this country it is hard to find a town that doesn't have both churches and mosques. This illustrates that, indeed, Bosnia and Herzegovina is at the crossroad of eastern and western civilizations. Despite the wars, the area of Bosnia and Herzegovina has survived for over five centuries as a very multi-religious part of the world.

The medieval Bosnian church is a good starting point for understanding contemporary Bosnia and Herzegovina. Inheriting the fierce self-reliant attitude from the indigenous Illyrian clans, the newly arrived Slavic tribes adopted their own form of Christianity. While most of Europe and the Balkans were under the influence of either of the two major Christian belief systems, geographically isolated Bosnia and Herzegovina celebrated a Christian god with many elements of paganism, and without the structure and hierarchy of the organized churches. Both Catholicism and Orthodoxy vied for power in the region, but the Bosnian Church was able to maintain its unique belief system for centuries.

The arrival of the Ottomans had a more substantial religious influence on the history of Bosnia and Herzegovina than the Orthodox and Catholic submission attempts of the previous period. The first Muslims came to the region in the mid-fifteenth century, and over the next one hundred and fifty years Bosnia saw a large portion of its population convert to Islam. In the sixteenth century a fourth group entered the region. Many of the Sephardic Jews that had been expelled from Spain in 1492 resettled in Sarajevo, Mostar, Travnik and other major Bosnian cities.

In Tito's Yugoslavia, most people strayed from their religious beliefs. Religious practice was allowed but frowned upon, secularism was encouraged and the religious leaders were chosen by the communist party. For a number of reasons, the breakdown of Yugoslàvia has caused a significant rise in the sense of religious belonging. First, people felt more at ease practicing their religions after the collapse of a country that was, essentially, proudly atheist. Second, a war and the suffering it causes often brings religion to the forefront. Third, this particular war was fought on ethnic lines and made many people more aware of their ethnic and thus religious identity. Fourth, and unfortunately, some of the religious revival can be attributed to nationalist agendas that use religion to inspire hatred.

Notwithstanding all the political rhetoric, the three main religious groups have influenced each other in the course of the five centuries in which they lived together. Consequently, and although many nationalists would deny it, Islam, Orthodoxy and Catholicism in Bosnia and Herzegovina are quite different from Islam, Orthodoxy and Catholicism anywhere else. Believers of each group often have more in common with their fellow-Bosnians than with their fellow-believers in other countries.

CULTURE

Some museums are good, but the exhibits of even the best ones do not match the power of the cultural manifestations that you will find everywhere in everyday life. Many of these cultural manifestations have this little twist that makes them unique to Bosnia and Herzegovina. Mosques around the world shy away from depicting living things, but the multicolored mosque in Travnik has elaborate flower scenes painted on the outside. The tombstones that line the countryside show roughly carved people with very large hands – something I have not seen anywhere else in the world. Many houses have no paintings at all, but many others have paintings covering their walls three rows high. Order a plate of meat or fish for a group of people and you will get an artfully composed and humorous mountain of niceties.

In Bosnia and Herzegovina, concepts are pursued until the very end. You see it in literature, where themes are considered from every possible side before the story goes on. You see it in the eye for detail when people dress up. You see it in the composition and variety of a mixed grill. You see it in the copper market in Ferhadija, where anything made of metal – trays, coffee sets, and even bullets and mortars - can be turned into a piece of art.

On the other hand, simplicity is treasured. A Turkish table, an Egyptian tray or a Palestinian dress are all about complexity and detail. Not an inch of material is left uncarved, uncut, unembroidered. Bosnia and Herzegovina shares the same Ottoman heritage, but its tables, trays and attires look decidedly different. They focus on beauty, not complexity. No-Man's Land, the Oscar-winning movie about the war, illustrates that this ability to transmit no-frill messages is still very much alive. The entire war is reduced to three men in a trench.

Art

There are very few cave paintings in Europe older than 14,000 years. The carvings in the Badanj Caves in southern Herzegovina are among them. Closely followed by pottery and artfully sculpted figures (on display at the National Museum in Sarajevo), they are the oldest art yet discovered in Bosnia and Herzegovina.

More refined art forms were taken from the Greeks and the Romans. In the Hellenistic and Roman eras, the Daorsi tribe - ahead of the other tribes - sometimes sided with and was influenced by both. The Daorsi left Hellenistic town remnants and moulds from jewelers' workshops. They introduced the symbols of early Christianity to the region, and left behind beautiful basilicas and mosaics.

These Paleolithic, Neolithic, Hellenistic and Roman remains are interesting, but do not yet show Bosnia and Herzegovina's unique face. That face appears in the medieval times. A new script appears – bosančica – and there are the symbols and art forms of the Bosnian church. Perhaps the most inspiring of these are the engraved tombstones, stećci in Bosnian, that still dot the countryside. These stećci, with pagan and Christian symbols of earth, moon, family, animals, dance and crosses, form a permanent reminder of the early Slavs' creativity.

Four centuries of Ottoman rule had a profound impact on the region. The many Ottoman bridges, mosques, markets, houses, libraries, dervish convents, streets and trading route resting places still give the country a decidedly oriental feel. Many of these Ottoman treasures are outside or can be visited. In the same period, the Christians painted the frescoes, icons and paintings that can be seen in the country's many monasteries. The orthodox monasteries of Paprača, Lomnica, Dobričevo, Žitomislići and Trijebanj and the Catholic monasteries of Kraljeva Sutjeska, Fojnica, Kreševo, Olovo, Gorica and Toliša are all well worth a visit.

Contemporary art has been influenced by all that preceded it. The Ottoman heritage lives forth in the work of the copper, gold, silver and leather crafts, and in the paintings of Safet Zec (famous for his delicate paintings of the oriental feel of a European Bosnia) and Mersad Berber (who portrays Muslim life in works such as Chronicle About Sarajevo). Other painters such as Gabriel Jurkić and Karlo Mijić and the abstract work of Affan Ramić depict the natural wonders of the Bosnian landscape, demonstrating the intimate ties between man and nature.

The war shines through in much of the most recent work of artists around the country. Artists display expressions of resistance, hope and peace. Sculpture, paintings, graffiti and graphic design all portray the new generation's struggle to heal the wounds of the past and rid the collective consciousness of the lunacy of the war.

Film

Bosnia and Herzegovina has produced some of the finest films to come out of the former Yugoslavia. Even Emir Kusturica, the great filmmaker from Serbia, was born and raised here. The modern film scene has taken off with the production of Danis Tanović's No-Man's Land (Ničija zemlja), this country's first-ever Oscar winning movie. In this brilliant tragic comedy, a few opposing soldiers, stuck in an abandoned trench between frontlines, represent the entire war. All is lost. In the end, the last man is left to die, unseen by the media, while an incompetent international representative walks away claiming a successful operation. In the back you hear a Bosnian bedtime song. Go to sleep. All is well.

Other striking movies, mostly about the war, include Perfect Circle (Savršeni krug) by Ademir Kenović, Fuse (Gori vatra) by Pjer Žalica, Re-Make by Dino Mustafić, and Summer in the Golden Valley (Ljeto u zlatnoj dolini), the 2004 winner of the Rotterdam Film Festival Tiger award. One of the latest Bosnian film productions is "Kod amidže Idriza", written by Namik Kabil and directed by Pjer Žalica. The film is a magnificent depiction of the peculiar and pronounced details of a Muslim family from Sarajevo. The attention to detail – particularly Bosnian cuisine and the inability of males to express their emotions - makes it a slow film, but one you don't want to end. If true insight into the heart of a typical Sarajevo family interests you, go see this film.

Literature

Ever since Ottoman times, Bosnia and Herzegovina has been a country of books. Muslim scholars, Serbian priests and Franciscan monks all contributed to Bosnia and Herzegovina's literary tradition.

Throughout the centuries, what shone through most writings was a strong sense of patriotism, the spirit of self-reliance, and the moral issues related to the political and social abuses suffered by all three peoples.

The most important pre-20th century authors

Mustafa Ejubović	Islamic scholarly thought.
Ahmed Sudi	Islamic scholarly thought.
Fevzi Mostarac	Wrote the famous Bulbulistan in 18th-century Persian.
Mula Mustafa Bašeskija	Wrote a diary of life in Sarajevo in the last half of the 1700s. He wrote it in a unique Turkish dialect that was only spoken in Sarajevo.
Hasan Kaimija	A poet who gained popularity as a defender of common folk.
Fra Matija Divković	Wrote the first published book in bosančica in Bosnia and Herzegovina in 1611 (printed in Venice).
Brother Filip Lastrić	The best-known historian of the Bosna Srebrena province. He wrote books that preserved the heritage of the old Bosnian State.
Nicifor Dučić	An orthodox monk who published nine volumes of historical works.
Joanikije Pamučina	Portrayed folklore and history in the Glorious Martyrdom of the Virgin Hristina Rajković.
Gavro Vučković Krajišnik	Wrote Slavery in Freedom or Mirror of Justice in Bosnia and The Bloody Book of Brother Ante Knežević. Both books were banned by the Ottoman government.
Vaso Pelagić	This was the greatest of the 19th-century Bosnian Serb writers. He stood out not only for his literary skill but also as one of the sharpest thinkers and political figures of his time.
Ivan Franjo Jukić	This Franciscan from Banja Luka personified the freedom struggle and wrote great works in many genres reflecting the emancipation movement that dominated 19th-century life in Bosnia and Herzegovina.

In the early twentieth century, many newspapers were established and Bosnian writers were fully exposed to European thought for the first time. After more than four centuries of Ottoman and Austrian rule, a struggle for national identity dominated the literature of this period. It was this struggle that had polarizing effects on the future of Bosnia. On the one hand it paved the way for the union of the southern Slavs. On the other hand it created ethnic rifts amongst the Slavs through the intensity of the nationalist voices which emerged. Ivo Andrić began his writing career in this period.

Alongside the nationalist fervor was the liberal movement of writers in The Comrades Book. This left-wing movement, with a passion for the social issues of the time, produced famous writers such as Novak Šimić, Hasan Kikić and Mak Dizdar. They were catalysts for the cultural revolution of the second half of the 20th century.

The greatest writers in Bosnia's history emerged post World War II in socialist Yugoslavia. Ivo Andrić continued his literary domination in the Bridge over the Drina, Travnik Chronicles and The Damned Yard. In 1961 he was awarded the Nobel Prize for Literature. Soon after, Mak Dizdar and Meša Selimović published two of Bosnia's most famous pieces: Stone Sleeper and Death and the Derviš. In the late sixties yet more masterpieces were published: Nedžad Ibrišimović's Ugursuz, Vitomir Lukić's Album, Skender Kulenović's first book of sonnets, and Branko Ćopić's book of stories The Blue Mallow Garden.

In post-war Bosnia the leading literary thinkers are Aleksandar Hemon, Nenad Veličković, Faruk Šehić, Dario Džamonja, Dževad Karahasan and Marko Vešović. Philosopher and writer Ivan Lovrenović offers one of the most insightful and objective viewpoints in Bosnian intellectual circles. For moving war accounts, read Miljenko Jergović's Sarajevo Marlboro and Zlata Maglajlić's Zlata's Diary. There are many others. They are now scattered across the globe, but their themes and inspiration tend to remain close to home.

The books of many of the writers mentioned here have been translated into English. Some of these books are available at the few bookshops in the country that have a sizeable English language selection.

Music

There are countries where a group of people who spend the evening together enjoy themselves talking or dancing. In Bosnia and Herzegovina, people tend to sing. For an outsider, it is a joy to watch. After an hour or so, somebody starts a 'sevdalinka', and the tone of the evening has been set: there is no more talking from that moment onwards. Instead, songs come and go, with or without instruments, for hours and hours. In just one voice, everybody sings the same nostalgic folk songs about life before the war. And everybody seems to know them all.

Most of this folk music traces its origins to Ottoman times and combines oriental elements with the popular heritage of Bosnia and Herzegovina. Most of these songs are songs of love and tragedy. They helped to get through turbulent times.

The sounds of the highlanders are equally fascinating. The music of the Dinaric shepherds has echoed through the mountain valleys for centuries. This type of mountain yodel is called ojkanje and is a mixed melody of male and female 'oi' sounds. Highlanders have always celebrated in open fields with the 'gluho kolo' or deaf dance. The villages' young bachelors and girls gather for a large circle dance accompanied by song. This ceremony continues through the night. It is often the setting for courting.

Then there is the ganga, a deep, non-instrumental, chant-like music most often sung by Croat men in Herzegovina. There is the Serbian gusle, a type of banjo, that accompanies century-old stories. There are the šargija instruments of the northwest of the country, and there is the Persian saz that most commonly accompanies traditional music in the cities. It's all unique to this region, and it's all equally tantalizing.

There is contemporary music as well. Famous groups from the old Yugoslavia are still held in high regard and their songs still crowd the airwaves. Groups like Bijelo dugme, Zabranjeno pušenje, Indexi and Crvena jabuka represent the climax of Yugoslav 1980s rock. Yesterday's and today's most famous pop stars are probably Dino Merlin and Kemal Monteno. With very different musical styles, they both enjoy huge popularity with young and old.

Sarajevo is the centre of Bosnia and Herzegovina's modern music scene but there are great bands from Mostar, Tuzla and Banja Luka as well. Mostar Sevdah Reunion is a magnificent band with a smooth mix of jazz, blues and a touch of tradition. Jazz bands and clubs have become increasingly popular and every November Sarajevo hosts a great International Jazz Festival. Digital music has hit the scene with Adi Lukovac i Ornamenti and others. But the tradition of rock and alternative music never died, and groups like Knock-Out, Kiks, Tifa, Sikter, and Protest still attract big crowds and play at venues throughout the country. Skroz and Dubioza kolektiv are the most popular new emerging bands.

Classical music, *by Keziah Conrad*

Sarajevans often pride themselves on sophisticated cultural tastes, including an appreciation for high-quality classical music. This music represents civilization, a link with the wider Western world—but more than that, it signifies beauty, passion, life, hope in the face of the darkest night. Many outsiders are familiar with the story of Vedran Smailović, a cellist in the Sarajevo Philharmonic Orchestra, who defiantly played on the streets and in ruined buildings while bombs and bullets rained down. Musicians have been a crucial part of the restoration of Sarajevo, giving voice to suffering, offering healing through beauty, taking part in projects that cross borders and lead toward reconciliation.

Three institutions are prominent in Sarajevo's classical music scene: the National Theater (with its Philharmonic Orchestra, Opera and Ballet), the Music Academy of Sarajevo University, and "JU Sarajevo Art", which coordinates performances of artists from Bosnia and Herzegovina and beyond. Sarajevo's National Theater opened in 1921, and since that time has been the scene of thousands of theatrical and musical performances. In 2004, musical events produced by the National Theater have included Mozart's *Requiem*, Orff's *Carmina Burana*, Beethoven's 5th Symphony, Verdi's *Nabucco*, Horozić's *Hasanaginica*, and a world premiere of Čavlović's opera *The Women of Srebrenica*. Sarajevo

Art organizes the annual summer festival Baščaršian Nights and an ongoing program of performances by local and international artists.

A range of amateur choirs and cultural societies perform regularly around the country. Several of these, such as Pontanima Interreligious Choir and the women's ensembles Gaudeamus and Allegra, have earned international recognition for their musicianship. Other groups include the choirs of the Cathedral, the Orthodox Church, and the Islamic *medresa* (school of theology).

Classical music in Bosnia and Herzegovina faces severe underfunding and a demoralizing lack of resources that has forced many prominent musicians to leave—but many others have stayed and are still working with passion and talent. Visiting artists and audience members often observe that musicians from this country have an electric energy and striking depth of feeling that is not easy to find elsewhere. Perhaps this is the product of artistry honed by suffering; a living vibrancy that arises out of intimate experience with death.

HISTORY

The history of the region of the former Yugoslavia has, for many, been a bewildering subject. Perhaps the most important thing to keep in mind while trying to fit the pieces of the Bosnian puzzle into a coherent context, is that the nationalist sentiments that were born at the end of the nineteenth century and are alive today, do not reflect the life and sentiments of the tiny, isolated communities of this country from the seventh to thirteenth centuries. The 'mental baggage' that is carried today by Serbs, Croats or Muslims can simply not be applied to a population which previously held no affiliation to a national or ethnic identity. The Orthodox from eastern Herzegovina did not wave a Serbian flag, the Catholics from Bosna srebrena did not have dreams of coming under Zagreb's rule, and the converted Muslim community had no aspirations to create a European Mecca in the heart of Bosnia. It is largely unknown whether the original Slav settlers, well into the Middle Ages, even referred to themselves at all as Serbs or Croats. All too often history is the story of kings and queens, conquerors and defenders, and provides little if any understanding of the life of the ordinary people. The early Slav tribes never engaged in bitter debates or wars over their Serbian or Croatian belonging; they lived in peace with each other, spoke the same language and worshipped the same god. Outside influences often divided communities but the impetus for such divisions never came from within.

In the historical context of Bosnia and Herzegovina much is still argued over, both domestically and internationally. What no one can debate, however, is today's rightful claim of all the peoples of Bosnia and Herzegovina to call this their home. Serbs, Croats and Bosniacs (the term used for Bosnian Muslims, identifying nationality and not religion) can confidently say that their homeland is Bosnia and Herzegovina and that they have been here for many, many generations. Claiming rightful ownership of one group over another from a historical perspective, with all its complexities, is simply an impossibility.

Ancient History

The territory of Bosnia and Herzegovina is profusely scattered with remnants of human life that spans the period from the Paleolithic age to the emergence of the Illyrian clan alliances.

Research into the Stone Age indicates that the northern parts of Bosnia and Herzegovina near the Bosna, Ukrina and Usora rivers were the most developed at that time. The leap from Neanderthal man in the middle Paleolithic, to the homo sapiens of the Late Paleolithic is signified by the first cave drawing of that period, found in Badanj Cave near Stolac in Herzegovina. This rare sample is dated at 12,000BC and there have been similar finds in only three other locations: Spain, France and Italy. The end of the Paleolithic Age saw tremendous climatic change, changes so drastic that much of human life disappeared from this area until about 4,000BC.

After this long, dark Mesolithic period a rich Neolithic culture developed in the third millennium BC. Conditions were ideal for the formation of settlements that developed a new kind of social organization and enjoyed over a millennium of continuity. Many of the fine pottery and arts and crafts of this age are on display in the National Museum in Sarajevo. This highly skilled culture signified a golden age where spiritual life was matched by creative talent. The ancient settlement of Butmir, presently a suburb south of Sarajevo at the base of Igman Mountain, can alone testify to the craftsmanship achieved in that territory by Neolithic man. This unique Neolithic culture disappeared from Bosnia and Herzegovina without a trace somewhere between the third and second millennia BC.

A great metamorphosis swept across the Balkans in a movement that began with the arrival of nomadic tribes from the Black Sea steppes. With their arrival to the Balkans came a new Copper Age. This Aeneolithic period saw a parallel development of stone and metal. The use of metal became increasingly valuable for weapon making, as well-armed tribes from west Pannonia expanded south and southeast towards the end of the second millennium. Wars became more frequent, and Bosnia became very popular for the sanctuary its deep valleys, thick forests and rugged mountains provided.

Illyrians

The first few centuries of the first millennium BC in Bosnia and Herzegovina, as throughout the entire western Balkan Peninsula, saw the gradual creation of a broad ethnic and cultural foundation. From the tribes belonging to the Iron Age culture emerged an ethnic group that history has collectively named the Illyrians.

The Illyrian tribes settled across a large swathe of the western Balkans from the Adriatic Coast in the west to the river Morava in the east, and from present day Albania in the south to the Istrian Peninsula in what today is northwest Croatia. These loosely bound tribes began to form new territorial and economic ties in the middle of the first millennium BC. This process appears to have been the most profound amongst the southern Illyrian tribes, including those tribes of present day Bosnia and Herzegovina.

The Celtic migration inland and the Greek colonies established on the Adriatic Coast in the 4th Century BC, marked a new and painful chapter in Illyrian history. These events brought about significant cultural and spiritual change. It also increased the desire of the Roman Empire to expand and conquer these areas.

The Romans attacked in 229BC, first capturing the islands and crushing the Illyrian navy. In 168BC the famous Illyrian king Gentius was defeated and this gave the Romans a stronghold on Illyrian soil. The inland tribes of Illyria, however, put up a ferocious fight and it took a century and a half of the Romans' best commanders and military forces to defeat the defiant clans. Finally, from 35-33BC, under the direct command of Emperor Octavian, the Roman army launched a major attack that, after the Emperor himself was seriously wounded from a guerilla attack, forced the surrender of the Dalmati clan. The coastal clans were by and large conquered by the overwhelming size of the Roman army.

In the last 'battle royal' for the inland territories held by the Illyrian tribes in what is the heart of present day Bosnia, the clan alliances staged what is known as the *Batonian Uprising*. Two namesakes of large Illyrian tribes united to fend off the invaders. Panicked by the rumors that there were '800,000 insurgents, including 200,000 elite warriors and 9,000 horsemen', Emperor Augustus sent two of his top commanders, Tiberius and Germanicus, to subdue and conquer the fierce and stubborn Illyrians. The fighting went on for years, with both sides exchanging defeats and victories. The last Illyrian stronghold to fall was the citadel at Vranduk near the central Bosnian city of Zenica. According to Roman records, when the Illyrian leader Batan surrendered, the Illyrian women, holding their children, threw themselves into the fire to avoid being captured and enslaved. The Romans incorporated the two Illyrian provinces of Pannonia and Dalmatia into their empire. Some extremely isolated remnants of Illyrian tribes probably survived and eventually assimilated with the Slavs when they arrived in the 7th century.

There are still a few archeological sites that mark the Illyrian civilization in Bosnia and Herzegovina. Many of the Illyrian fortifications were expanded upon by the Romans and later by the Bosnian aristocracy and the Ottomans. New research, however, has uncovered a fascinating aspect of Illyria. At Vranduk in central Bosnia, Blagaj near the Buna River in Herzegovina and on the Cyclopean walls at Osanići near Stolac, finds have indicated that the culture of antiquity came long before the Romans, most likely in Hellenistic form. Osanići was home to the Daorsi tribe and recent archeological findings point to a third century BC link to a northerly extension of the great Hellenistic civilization.

Much of Illyrian culture will forever remain a mystery but one cannot deny the spiritual and cultural impact it has had, even almost two millennia after their disappearance.

Ancient Illyricum

With the fall of the Illyrian clan alliances to the Romans, the territory of present day Bosnia and Herzegovina became part of the vast Roman Empire.

The early period of Roman occupation was peaceful and stable. There were, of course, some tribes who rejected Roman rule but for the most part the efficient Romans quickly set aim at taming Illyricum to cater to the Empire's needs. A Roman administration was established and the task of building roads, mining for iron, gold, lead and rock and mobilizing a large labor force and military were the first priorities. The Illyrians were actively recruited into the Roman army.

The most populated areas continued to be the Empire's regional centers. By the third century AC Illyricum had flourished into a proper Roman province. Its people had equal standing within the Empire and could even aspire to political office. Although Christianity was introduced and largely accepted, elements of Illyrium pagan beliefs were maintained and passed on.

With the disintegration of the western Empire in the fifth century much of the Illyrian lands fell into the hands of the Ostrogoths. The Illyrians again enjoyed a period of relative peace and stability but by the mid-6th century the eastern Empire was able to regain most of the Illyrian lands. As the Roman Empire declined new attacks occurred on the northern frontiers, this time from the Avars and Slavs.

After several centuries of drastic social change in Europe a mélange of cultures made their mark on present day Bosnia and Herzegovina. Basilicas from the late Roman period can be found as their use was continued by the new settlements of Slavs. Remains can be found in Čapljina, Blagaj and Ljubuški in Herzegovina; Breza, Zenica, Travnik and Kiseljak in central Bosnia; and Banja Luka and Mrkonjić Grad in the northwest of the country.

The Slavs

With the fall of the western Empire the new era in Bosnia and Herzegovina was largely dominated by the Slavs. From the sixth century onwards sizeable Slav migration flows came from the east. The Avars gradually retreated to Pannonia but the Slavs remained in their new homeland. It is this ethnic group that most of present day Bosnia and Herzegovina's ethnic make-up is based upon.

Historical evidence of the first centuries of Slav settlements in the area of Bosnia and Herzegovina is practically non-existent. The first recorded evidence of Bosnia and Herzegovina under the Slavs dates from the tenth century. Several centuries later a Byzantine writer stated that 'Bosnia is not a vassal state but is independent, the people lead their own life and rule themselves.'

Graveyards have become the most important source of information about the culture of this time. Archeological digs in older necropolises have unearthed locally made jewellery and weapons from the Slav period. A unique aspect of this time was the development of skilled work with stone. This art would later surface in what is seen today as a national trademark of Bosnia and Herzegovina – the stećak (plural stećci). These medieval tombstones were elaborately carved with drawings depicting Christian and pagan beliefs. Stećci date from the eleventh to the thirteenth centuries and can be found today at dozens of locations all over Bosnia and Herzegovina. These tombstones are unique to this part of the world.

Medieval Bosnia

The early Middle Ages placed the southern Slavs in a very precarious position – wedged between the two great cultural bodies of eastern and western Christianity. Both Byzantium and Rome set out to influence the political and religious structure of this crossroads region. The geographical position of the southern Slavs became an important factor in the eleventh century split between the Orthodox and Catholic churches. Both churches asserted their influences and left a permanent mark on the region's cultural history.

The spiritual culture that developed in medieval Bosnia was very similar to that of its Illyrian predecessors. There was a large degree of cultural resistance and fierce independence that resulted in a creative mold of Christianity. In a relatively inaccessible and isolated area emerged what was to be a unique form of Christianity in medieval Europe – the Bosnian church. Whilst still influenced by the great divide and spread of Orthodoxy and Catholicism the Bosnian church, along with its own alphabet – *bosančica* (similar to both Glagolithic and Cyrillic) - flourished in the medieval Bosnian state. In an era that saw Europe dominated by religious exclusiveness, Bosnia was able to maintain a high level of secularism in all spheres of life.

Cultural development in medieval Bosnia

Written records don't show how the ordinary persons lived, what lifestyle they enjoyed, and what cultural heritage developed in medieval Bosnia. What we do know is that many unique forms of language, art, literature, and worship evolved in Bosnia during the Middle Ages.

The key to Bosnia's wealth was its copper, silver, lead, gold and other natural resources. Copper and silver were mined at Kreševo and Fojnica in central Bosnia; lead was mined in Olovo to the northeast of Sarajevo; and gold, silver and lead in were mined in Zvornik on the River Drina. The most significant and productive area in all of Bosnia and Herzegovina was the silver mine at Srebrenica. A large working class developed around this industry, some of which can still be found today.

During the Middle Ages Bosnia became a very important trading route. Merchants from both east and west moved and traded their goods through or in Bosnian territory. Trading towns and routes sprung up or rejuvenated in Visoko, Jajce, Travnik, Goražde and Livno. Many locals became involved in trade, particularly with Ragusa (Dubrovnik). Bosnia and Dubrovnik today still share close cultural ties.

A unique alphabet evolved in medieval Bosnia. Cyrillic and Glagolithic had been introduced in the tenth century and a special form of Cyrillic developed during the middle-ages. Glagolithic and Cyrillic were used simultaneously for some time, both copying texts and manuscripts from each other. The use of these two alphabets slowly merged into one - Bosnian Cyrillic or *bosančica.* It became the most commonly used alphabet in later medieval times.

Whereas most literature in medieval Europe came from clergy and monasteries, Bosnian writings were remarkably secular. The most famous of these is the Kulin Charter of 1189, written to the people of Dubrovnik. This was the first official act written in the national language of the Slavic south. Many documents show that it was not only the nobility but merchants and craftsmen who reached a relatively high level of literacy. There are, however, also many religious documents from this time. Examples include the Cyrillic *Miroslav Missal*, produced by the Duke of Hum in the 12th century, the *Divoš Tihoradić Gospel* from the 14th century and the *Čajniče Gospel* which is the only medieval codex still in existence in Bosnia today. These manuscripts used a wealth of human and animal miniatures all drawn in a unique south Slav style. The Franciscan monastery in Kraljeva

Sutjeska possesses some of the earliest written works and the first bible, complete with the *bosančica* alphabet. They can be viewed in the museum and library in this small town in central Bosnia.

Art took many forms in medieval Bosnia. Silver, gold, bronze and copper were used, particularly in the 14th and 15th centuries, for jewellery making, costumes, coins, bowls, and other artifacts. Many of the designs resemble Romanesque-Gothic styles, some with an eastern mystical flavor. The most important art of medieval Bosnia, though, was the stonework of the *stećci* (gravestones). These unique gravestones from Bosnia and Hum are not found anywhere else in Europe.

In different styles, these *stećci* portray crosses, swords, symbols of purity, and anthropomorphic symbols (dance, traditional attire, sacred symbols, deer, horses). The Bosnian Cyrillic script showed its most artistic face on these *stećci*. But the most remarkable trait of the *stećci* is their poetic and philosophical power. They stand apart from any known conventional European burial rites. They are found mostly in Bosnia and Herzegovina but there are also *stećci* in Dalmatia, the Croatian hinterland, western Serbia and Montenegro – all within the boundaries of the former Bosnian State. This art form continued into Ottoman times and well into the 16th century, with some of the later *stećci* including Islamic symbols.

Bosnia and Herzegovina is a living gallery of the stone art of the middle-ages. Over 60,000 *stećci* tombstones are dotted throughout the country with the largest necropolis at Radimlja near the Herzegovinian town of Stolac. Mak Dizdar, the most famous of Bosnian poets, wrote frequently of the *stećci* and their meaning in *Kameni spavač*, the *Stone Sleeper*. Whether or not his interpretations of the *stećci* are right, they remain a national symbol of Bosnia and Herzegovina.

It should be well noted that most of medieval European history does not see it fit to mention much of the contributions of women during this time. The mainly male dominant and patriarchal depiction of this era is to say the least unfair – as women have always made significant contributions in art, agriculture, family life, and even male dominated politics. The authors do not wish to exclude women by any means but have simply been unable to unearth their major contributions of this time. What we do know is that women in the region of Bosnia and Herzegovina at this time were not persecuted as witches as were their counterparts in much of western Europe.

Ottoman rule

In the summer of 1463 the Ottoman army, after years of penetration into Bosnian territory, captured the Bosnian banate and the region around Sarajevo. These lands would be in more or less firm Ottoman control for the next four centuries. Many of the gains in the northern half of Bosnia, however, were reversed by King Mathias of Hungary. He established a northern banate under Hungarian rule and named the Bosnian 'ban' King of Bosnia. The kingdom slowly dwindled as Ottoman incursions wore down the resistance, and by the 1520s the kingdom's capital, Jajce, came under constant siege until it fell in 1528.

Herzegovina also succeeded in repelling the Ottomans for some time after 1463. Herceg Stjepan Vukčić held most of Herzegovina for the next two years, until another swarming invasion sent him into exile in Novi (later named Herceg-Novi in his honor), Montenegro. His son Vlatko attempted to enlist the help of the Hungarians and Venetians but internal strife with local noblemen and neighboring Ragusa enabled the Ottomans to take a strong hold by the 1470s, and in 1482 the last fortress in Herzegovina was overrun.

The Ottomans conquered territories, particularly in the north towards Europe, not to convert the inhabitants, but for the land, for acquiring new conscripts for further Ottoman gains, and for the taxes the Empire could impose to wage these wars. Besides conquering Bosnia and Herzegovina, Mehmed II destroyed the Venetian army in Greece, began making incursions into Moldavia and Hungary, and was on the verge of launching a full scale invasion of Italy when he died in 1481. His successor, Bayezit II, continued consolidating Ottoman gains. Suleyman the Magnificent's rule from 1520-1566 managed to reduce Hungary to the status of a vassal territory and the Ottomans came inches away from capturing Vienna. The 1533 peace treaty with Austria established a long and static confrontation line between the Hapsburg and Ottoman Empires. Each side spent years building up their respective frontier zones, thus assuring that Bosnia's borders did not see heavy military activity until the Sultan waged war on the Hapsburgs in 1566. Military campaigns continued from 1593 to 1606. The Ottoman presence in Bosnia was a military enterprise from where major offensives against the Hapsburgs were launched.

In the course of 150 years, more and more of Bosnia's inhabitants converted to Islam. The Islamicization of the Bosnian population is possibly the most distinctive and maybe the most important event in its history. There was, and still is, a lot of controversy surrounding this issue, with most arguments being based on myth and folklore. Although one will still find today bitter 'memories' of 'forced' conversion, the process as a whole did not largely come by force or through war.

While the evidence available does not prove that there was a policy of forced conversions, this is not to say that there was no persecution and oppression of Christians. The Orthodox Church, falling under the jurisdiction of the Ottoman Empire, was an accepted institution. The Catholic Church, the church of the enemy Austrians, was treated with a heavier hand. In the geographical territory of Bosnia at the time of the Ottoman conquest, there were few Orthodox communities. They grew in size during the Ottoman occupation. Conversely, there were an estimated 35 Franciscan monasteries in Bosnia and Herzegovina before the invasion, but by the mid-1600s only ten remained.

The religious practices of both the Bosnian Christians and Muslims point to a mystical convergence of the two faiths. Even today, Christians and Muslims share the same superstitions in the power of amulets, with many Muslims having them blessed by Franciscan monks. Many holy days and festivals were celebrated by both religious communities. 'Muslim' ceremonies were often conducted in Christian churches and masses were held in front of the Virgin Mary to cure or ward off illness. There are records of Christians calling for Muslim dervishes to read verses from the Qu'ran to cure or bless them. It is quite clear that a synthesis of diverging beliefs occurred in Bosnia and Herzegovina, where 'all sects meet on a common basis of secular superstition.'

Most of Bosnia and Herzegovina's present day cities and towns were created during the Ottoman period. A focus on building towns and constructing roads and bridges to connect these towns brought the whole country, for the first time, into an urbanized sphere. Never before had any central administration effectively embarked on a vision of building a country. Islamic art and culture added a remarkable aspect to life in Bosnia and Herzegovina. Unlike the often brutal feudal systems seen elsewhere in Europe at that time, the Ottoman Empire allowed the Orthodox Church and the new Jewish community to enjoy growth and prosperity.

A small community of Sephardic Jews who had been expelled from Spain in 1492 settled in Sarajevo, Travnik and Mostar, and was tolerated by the Ottomans. Jewish merchants quickly established themselves in the textile and silk trades. This tradition would stand until the destruction of the Jewish community in the Second World War. They were skilled metal workers and it is believed that the Anatolian Jews greatly advanced Ottoman weaponry. For this priceless gift it is said that the Jews were given their own mahala in Sarajevo near the central market. Several synagogues and a hram were built. From an early stage after their arrival, the Jews of Bosnia and Herzegovina played an important role in the cultural and religious life of the cities where they settled.

The decline of the Ottoman Empire

A major Ottoman defeat at the hands of the Austrians in 1683 signaled a drastic decline in the Empire. In 1697 Eugene of Savoy advanced on Bosnia and reached Sarajevo. Sarajevo was put to the torch and most of the town went up in flames. When he retreated many Catholics left with his army for fear of reprisals. This decimated the Catholic population and only three Franciscan monasteries remained open. The frontier lands in the Krajina were in constant conflict, and unrest in eastern Herzegovina along the Montenegrin border became commonplace

At the turn of the nineteenth century Napoleon and France defeated Austria and took over Venetia, Istria and Dalmatia. Austria again declared war on France in 1809 and by 1813 Austria ruled those areas again. The biggest threat, however, was no longer the Austrians but the powerful rebellions to the east in Serbia. Large-scale revolts took place in which Slav Muslims were massacred. The Ottomans granted Serbia a greater amount of autonomy in 1815. By the end of the Napoleonic wars it became clear to Istanbul that the Empire was so weak that it would collapse without aggressive reform. Now fighting battles on all fronts it was too difficult for the Ottomans to reestablish control of Bosnia. Bosnia's local governors and military leaders looked for more autonomy and began making demands to the Ottoman authorities. Many local militias offered the Ottomans military assistance but with strict demands on self-rule and insisting that taxes levied by the Empire be waived. Christians and Muslims alike were seeking sweeping reforms within the Empire. A final blow was struck in a massive revolt that lasted three years from 1875 to 1878. This revolt effectively ended Ottoman rule in Bosnia and Herzegovina. Russia had declared war on the Ottoman Empire in 1877, and the earlier plans of the Austrians and Russians would soon become reality. By October 20, 1878 the total occupation of Bosnia and Herzegovina was complete. A new era under Austro-Hungarian rule began.

Austro-Hungarian rule

The Congress of Berlin redrew the map of the Balkans and approved the Austro-Hungarian occupation of Bosnia and Herzegovina in 1878, and the

Austro-Hungarians wasted no time in establishing their rule.

By holding the territory of Bosnia and Herzegovina, Austro-Hungary acquired great economic and market potential. More importantly, it enabled the empire to effectively establish an opposition to Russian influence in the Balkans. They were able to keep a close watch on Serbia and could begin 'experimenting' on an even greater ambition – expansion to the east. These factors shaped Austro-Hungarian policy in Bosnia and Herzegovina. Austro-Hungarian rule allowed the feudal system, however backwards and outdated, to continue and govern everyday life. Meanwhile, progressive and modern measures in certain spheres of life were rapidly embarked upon.

The most visible changes under Austro-Hungarian occupation were the introduction of European styles of architecture, cuisine, behavior, and dress, and the population reshuffle. Lacking confidence in the native inhabitants, foreign officials, mainly Slav, assumed the administrative duties of governing the state. Large numbers of peasants from the Empire's other territories were brought into Bosnia and Herzegovina's already overwhelmingly peasant population. Muslims from Bosnia and Herzegovina emigrated south and east on a massive scale as the Empire implemented a policy of rebalancing the country's religious make-up.

Within the framework of a new colonial policy, widespread and rapid social change and national diversification occurred. These changes fueled national and political antagonisms so powerful that even the mighty Austro-Hungarian Empire could not keep them at bay. It was not so much an organized agenda of political affiliation but rather a spontaneous expression, largely by youth, of a revolutionary spirit. Nationalist agendas did arise in the beginning of the 20th century but the general resistance was more at a class level than at a national one. Acts of terrorism began when Bosnia and Herzegovina was officially annexed in 1908. In 1910, there was a failed assassination attempt on Emperor Franz Joseph. In the same year the governor of Bosnia and Herzegovina, general Marijan Varešanin, was shot, and in June 1914 a young Serbian nationalist by the name of Gavrilo Princip shot dead Prince Ferdinand and his pregnant wife on a bridge in Sarajevo. This event not only sparked the end of Austro-Hungarian rule in Bosnia and Herzegovina, but also led to the large political fallouts between the great powers that preceded the first battles of World War I.

Austro-Hungary's declaration of war on Serbia on July 28, 1914 carved deep wounds and strengthened aged alliances amongst the world powers. Bosnians and Herzegovinians were sent to fight against the regime that repressed them.

The Kingdom of Serbs, Croats, and Slovenes and the First Yugoslavia

Towards the end of WWI the Austro-Hungarians attempted to 'rearrange' the status of Bosnia and Herzegovina. The governor of Bosnia and Herzegovina, Baron Sarkotić, suggested to the Emperor that the country join with Croatia or be granted special autonomy under the Hungarian crown. As the war efforts continued to falter towards the end of 1918, the idea of Bosnia and Herzegovina remaining under Austro-Hungarian rule was completely abandoned and talks of the creation of a Yugoslav state began. The leader of the Bosnian Muslims, Mehmed Spaho, had the task of uniting the divided loyalties of the Muslim populations. Although some disparities still existed amongst the Muslims he declared the Muslims of Bosnia and Herzegovina were in favor of a Yugoslav state. National Councils were formed, first in Zagreb and then in Bosnia and Herzegovina, renouncing the rule of the Hapsburgs in countries formerly under Austro-Hungarian authority. Days later, Croatia, Bosnia and Herzegovina and Slovenia joined with the Kingdom of Serbia to form the Kingdom of Serbs, Croats, and Slovenes. Within this new kingdom, Croatia, as well as the Bosnian Muslims and Bosnian Croats, sought some sort of regional self-governance. The Kingdom of Serbia, supported by the Bosnian Serbs, did not feel for that and established a centralist style rule from Belgrade.

Resistance against the Serb domination mounted, and in 1932 the leader of the Croatian party, Vlatko Maček, issued a 'Resolution' calling for a return to democracy and the end of Serbian hegemony. The Slovenian and Bosnian leaders followed suit with similar statements and all three were subsequently arrested. Their arrests did not go down well, and in 1934 King Aleksandar was assassinated. A year later his successor, Prince Paul, ordered new elections. The resulting loose new alliance lasted a shaky four years and ended when a Serbian minister asserted to parliament in a speech that the 'Serb policies will always be the policies of this house and this government.' Later that evening five key ministers resigned and the government imploded.

Hitler had by now begun advancing on Czechoslovakia, and his devout admirer Ante Pavelić in Italy was pushing for the break-up of Yugoslavia. It was apparent that there was a desperate need for the Serbs to bring the Croats back on board and to find a solution the Croats would accept. Cvetković and Maček met and began discussing the restructuring of the national territories, which would include giving Croatia some political power of its own. The new solution carved-up Bosnia giving some parts to Croatia and leaving other parts to be devoured by Serbia. The Bosnian Muslim leader Spaho died during these negotiations and his successor Džafer Kulenović sought the creation of a separate banate for Bosnia. His requests were ignored as much of the banates not absorbed into the new Croatia banates had a majority Serb population who wanted to maintain close ties with the remaining banates dominated by Serbia.

These debates continued until the pressure asserted from the German Reich became too much to bear for the Yugoslav government. With Hitler on their border and the Italians already in Greece, Prince Paul realized the impossibility of protection from Great Britain and signed the Axis pact in Vienna on March 25, 1941. When the Yugoslav delegation returned, the Prince was ousted in a bloodless coup and a new government of national unity was formed. The new government tried to continue a conciliatory policy towards Germany but ten days later massive bombing raids on Belgrade began, and Yugoslavia was invaded by German, Bulgarian, Hungarian and Italian forces. The 'resistance' lasted eleven days, after which the Yugoslav army surrendered to the German High Command.

The Second World War

After the defeat of the Yugoslav army, Yugoslavia was divided between the Axis powers. Its territories became important for communication and supplies of natural resources and labor to fight the Allied powers. The Axis powers were focused on defeating the Allied forces and were not prepared for the war against the Yugoslav resistance movements, and the two civil wars that ensued.

Before the end of the blitzkrieg the Germans had proclaimed a new 'Independent State of Croatia' (known as NDH), which also engulfed all of Bosnia and Herzegovina. Croatian extremists conducted a war largely against the Serb populations in Croatia and Bosnia and Herzegovina. There was also war between the two main resistance groups – the *četnici*, who were Serbs loyal to the monarchy, and the communist partisans that enlisted Serbs, Muslims and Croats.

Under the leadership of Josip Broz, or Tito, the partisans envisioned a communist victory over the Germans and a social revolution that would create a post-war communist state. Tito was a Stalin loyalist whose revolutionary ideology attracted a population that was weary and worn by nationalist agendas.

Two of the most crucial battles of WWII in Yugoslavia took place in Bosnia and Herzegovina. In the early months of 1943 the most epic battle for the partisans began – the Battle of the Neretva. A surprise counter offensive was launched by the partisans in the direction of Herzegovina and Montenegro. In retreat from battles in the Krajina region the partisans reached the Neretva River with 4,000 wounded and many more villagers who had joined the partisans in fleeing from German attacks. With over 20,000 *četnik* troops on one side and Axis forces on the other, Tito sabotaged the bridge at Jablanica, leading the enemy to believe the partisans had changed course. He ordered the bridge to be destroyed and improvised a wooden footbridge. All the wounded were brought across and the footbridge destroyed, thus deceiving the German forces. The partisans now faced the *četnik* army, and in a fierce battle the *četniks* were wiped out. Tito and the partisans were able to secure a safe passage to Montenegro. The remains of the bridge can still be seen today in Jablanica and there is a full account of the battle at the museum in that town.

By May the Germans had begun preparations for the largest campaign of the war. Over 100,000 troops, backed by air power, surrounded the outnumbered partisans in the mountainous region near the River Sutjeska in eastern Bosnia. The Partisans attempted to break through to the eastern border with Montenegro and over 7,000 partisans lost their lives. Today Sutjeska is a National Park that pays tribute to the downed partisans.

Tito's Yugoslavia

Depending on who you talk to, Tito was either a monstrous communist dictator or a peacekeeping socialist visionary. The truth probably lies somewhere in the middle. At the end of WWII, Yugoslavia, like much of Europe, was a mess. Tito quickly introduced Stalinist methodology in running his new communist republic. His logic was that in order to plant the seeds of socialist ideology, nationalist sentiments must be uprooted and weeded out at all costs. This resulted in the death of what some estimate to be 250,000 Croats, Muslims and Serbs. The Department for the Protection of the People, Tito's secret police, arrested and often severely punished anyone who opposed 'brotherhood and unity', and in fact anyone they *thought* might threaten the new fragile state. The Croats were especially targeted, some having supported the ustaša and been followers of Ante Pavelić.

The Franciscan clergy in Herzegovina were also singled out, having been suspected of supporting the *ustaša* against the Partisans. Many churches were destroyed and monasteries shut down. Serbian *Četniks* were also seriously persecuted and many either left the country or retreated to isolated mountain areas. The Muslims were also served harsh punishments; executions of the Muslim intellectual elite were commonplace in the early years after the war. The courts of Islamic sacred law were suppressed, teaching of children in mosques became a criminal offense, women were forbidden to wear the veil and many Muslim cultural societies were forced to close.

In 1948 Stalin expelled Yugoslavia from the Cominform. At this time Tito quickly changed his platform from being a stark Stalinist to being a more open minded, independent and liberal socialist. By the mid-fifties, religious life in Yugoslavia improved, with new laws that allowed freedom of religion, although the state was mandated with directing and controlling these institutions.

Whereas the first half of the new Yugoslavia was built around establishing authority, rebuilding, and weeding out opposition, Yugoslavia in the 1960s and beyond brought about a kind of national renaissance. It is from this point on that people speak of the glorious days of Tito - when everyone had a job and there was free education. There were no homeless and people were free to travel around the world.

Massive changes to the infrastructure, particularly road systems, opened much of the impenetrable Bosnia and Herzegovina for the first time. The National Roads Launch of 1968 aimed at connecting every town in the country with asphalt roads. Almost a thousand schools and libraries were built. The library program was co-funded by Nobel Laureate Ivo Andrić. He donated half of his prize money for this project. Schools in rural areas and small villages were established as were small medical clinics or 'ambulanta.' The university system was expanded from Sarajevo to Banja Luka, Tuzla, Mostar, Zenica, and other major cities in Bosnia and Herzegovina.

Tito established and maintained good relations with both the United States and the Soviet Union and Yugoslavia received financial aid from both of them in a typical cold war 'tug-o-war.' New incentives by the communist party for 'self-management' within the republics gave the population a sense of pride and independence. For the average person in Bosnia and Herzegovina, life was good. People had jobs, relatively comfortable lifestyles and were free to travel and work abroad.

After Tito

After the death of Tito in 1980, Bosnia and Herzegovina continued to enjoy relative prosperity. The deepening crisis in Kosovo in the early eighties, however, gave further fuel to the Serbian nationalist cause. Dobrica Ćosić, a Serbian nationalist Communist, complained that 'one could witness among the Serbian people a re-ignition of the old historic goal and national idea – the unification of the Serbian people into a single state.' This statement led to his expulsion from the Central Committee. Ćosić also fiercely opposed the granting of national status to the Bosnian Muslims. Anti-Muslim, and for nationalist propaganda purposes, anti-Islamic, sentiment was fuel for the fire of Serbian nationalism.

By the mid-1980s, the economic situation in Yugoslavia began to deteriorate. Without the strong leadership of Tito, poor economic times gave further rise to nationalism. In 1987 inflation rose 120% and by the next year that rate had doubled. In the last few years of the eighties strikes and protests became commonplace. In 1989 strikes against the local party leaders in Vojvodina and Montenegro set the stage for the new leader of the Serbian Communists – Slobodan Milošević.

Milošević clearly had an agenda of transformation in Serbia and he quickly replaced party leaders with his own supporters. In March 1989, at Milošević's request, the Serbian Assembly passed a constitutional amendment that abolished the autonomy of Kosovo and Vojvodina. This was met by massive strikes in Kosovo that were violently dealt with by the Serbian security forces. In a general atmosphere of discontent among the masses, due to the worsening economic times, political finger pointing stirred a nationalist fury that few could have imagined. The Serbs could now either dominate Yugoslavia or break it up. Even at this point, however, few Bosnians saw the rise of nationalism or the deepening economic woes as a sign of war or disintegration. Life, for the most part, carried on as normal.

The break-up of Yugoslavia

The symbolic turning point in the collapse of Yugoslavia came in the summer of 1989 at Kosovo polje. Hundreds of thousands of Serbs gathered at this ancient battle-field to pay respects to Prince Lazar, who had been slain at this place in 1389 in battle against the Ottomans. In the weeks leading up to the ceremony the bones of the Prince toured Serbia, stirring the pot of unsettled scores in the minds of many Serbs. Milošević addressed those assembled saying that 'we are again engaged in battles and quarrels. They are not yet armed battles, but this cannot be ruled out yet.' His words clearly stuck a resounding chord and were met with thundering applause. Through careful nationalist rhetoric Milošević secured half of the eight votes in the federal government. He controlled Serbia, Montenegro, Kosovo and Vojvodina. In his eyes that left only the challenge of getting Macedonia on board to gain a majority and further implement constitutional change in favor of Serbian dominance.

With the fall of the Berlin wall came the unification of East and West Germany and the almost overnight collapse of the Soviet Union. Faced now with a struggling economy and the shift from a planned to a market economy, there were demands by the republics for more freedom and sovereignty from the federal government. The Serbian government attempted to block any movement toward the break-up of Yugoslavia. Talk of independence increased in Slovenia and Croatia in 1990, and at the 14th Congress of the League of Communists of Yugoslavia, President Slobodan Milošević issued a warning that republics seeking independence would face border changes on the assumption that anywhere a Serb lived was part of Serbia. This only fueled Croatian nationalism which had become more radical in the late eighties. As Milošević's power base expanded, the 'dream' of an independent Croatia became increasingly appealing to many Croats.

In Bosnia and Herzegovina, the Serbian propaganda machine shifted its focus from the *ustaša* hordes to the Islamic fundamentalist threat. In reality, Bosnia's Muslim population, especially after almost 50 years of socialism, was mainly secular and pro-Europe. Holding a 44% minority in the country they feared that both Serbian and Croatian lust to take Bosnia and Herzegovina would leave them nation-less.

As was done in Slovenia and Croatia, a referendum for independence was held in Bosnia and Herzegovina in March 1992. The Bosnian Croats and Muslims voted in favor, whilst a majority of the Serbian population boycotted the vote. With sixty-five per cent of Bosnia's population voting in favor, Bosnia and Herzegovina declared independence notwithstanding Serbian threats. The day the results were announced Serb paramilitary forces set up barricades and sniper posts near the parliament building in Sarajevo. Suddenly, the heavy artillery and tanks that had already surrounded Sarajevo and several other cities before the independence vote, were a very real threat.

On April 6, 1992 the European Union and the United Nations recognized Bosnia and Herzegovina as an independent state. On the same day the Yugoslav National Army and Serbian paramilitaries attacked Sarajevo. Tens of thousands of Sarajevans of all nationalities took to the streets to protest in front of the barricades. As the crowd peacefully marched toward the barricade a sniper from the hillside fired into the crowd, killing a woman from Sarajevo and a Muslim woman who had fled the fighting in Dubrovnik. This sparked the beginning of what would be a long and brutal campaign against Bosnia's non-Serb populations.

In less than a year Yugoslavia saw three of its six republics secede. Macedonia followed suit and a UN preventive force was sent to intersect any pending ambitions Serbia had on Macedonia. Serbia and Montenegro, together with the provinces of Vojvodina and Kosovo, were now all that remained of Yugoslavia

The conflict

There have been so many books written about this subject that the authors have decided to let the reader, if they so choose, to further research the conflict. For the sake of sparing this book from the dark days of the early 1990's we will skip the details of the war that flashed on our screens from 1992 to 1995. Although this issue is still a topic of heavy debate here it is clear that Bosnia and Herzegovina experienced the worst genocide on European soil since WWII. Addressing the truths of the war is a necessary process for healing – both by victim and aggressor, but we feel that this is not the place for this. In short, we have moved on from those days and hope our readers will too and fully experience the beauty of Bosnia and Herzegovina today.

What one rarely learns or reads about of conflicts such as this one is the 'other side of the coin.' A spirit of resistance and survival thrived during these times. Communities mobilized to help one another. An untapped strength and creativity was expressed through the war theatre in Sarajevo that put on plays for the duration the siege. The newspaper *Oslobođenje*, meaning Freedom, did not miss a single day of print despite the lack of paper and supplies. Cultural life did not die during these times, it flourished in the most defiant form of non-violent resistance. Bosnians walked through the hail of gunfire to have coffee with a friend and held a Miss Sarajevo beauty pageant in a basement during one of the worst periods of the war. The attempts to erase all material traces of Bosnia's Muslim and Islamic culture may have partially succeeded in the torching of libraries and razing of mosques, but the spirit of a multi-ethnic community never died. Hundreds of thousands of Bosnians – Muslim, Serb and Croat – lost their lives, some in the most horrific ways imaginable. And although in some circles the madness of ethnic purity still exists you will find that in most places in Bosnia today people are determined to live a normal life again, and to live together...as they always have.

Post-war Bosnia and Herzegovina

Difficult times and a long rehabilitation process followed the signing of the Dayton Peace Accords. Although progress and reform has come slow in the eyes of the local inhabitants, great strides have been made in the normalization of life in Bosnia and Herzegovina. In the early years after Dayton the peace was monitored and enforced by a large NATO presence. Sarajevo became the headquarters of the multi-national peacekeeping force and the Brits, Americans and French commanded their respective jurisdictions in the rest of the country with smaller NATO countries under their command. More importantly, electricity, food, and water returned to the beleaguered population. Shops were once again filled with European products and a massive reconstruction program began on a scale not seen since the Marshall Plan.

Freedom of movement between the entities was improved with the introduction of standardized car license plates. Registration plates after the war clearly stated which entity one was from, which often led to harassment and/or random violence. The return of refugees was a slower process and one that is still ongoing. Large numbers of refugees and displaced persons have returned to their rightful homes, but many remain in third countries or internally displaced within Bosnia and Herzegovina.

Government reform was and still is a painful process. The nationalist parties that led the country into war still ruled in the immediate years after Dayton. The new constitution stipulates the full equal rights and representation of all three peoples of Bosnia and Herzegovina, giving even minority groups an unprecedented voice in government. The presidency is not a one-person position but rather a three-person consortium with rotating powers to the Serb, Croat, and Bosniac delegates. The circus of establishing an equally balanced government was no less than a poorly constructed jigsaw puzzle. Ministry positions were given to political parties regardless of the background or competency of the individuals involved. Appointees stuck hard to party lines instead of nation building. Corruption was rampant and became an inherent part of the system, and has proved very difficult to uproot. This did little to improve the power of a centralized government, nor help begin the process of reconciliation.

Bosnia and Herzegovina was assigned an internationally mandated governing body to oversee the rebuilding process, called the Office of the High Representative (OHR). Most Bosnians viewed the NATO forces as peaceful and necessary occupiers and have a similar opinion of the OHR. The powers of the OHR are broad and sweeping, so much so that in essence they play an ad hoc protectorate role. Free and fair elections were implemented by the Office for Security and Cooperation in Europe (OSCE). The elections in 2002 were the first elections to be fully implemented by the local government. Previously elected officials were only able to serve two-year terms that were often counter productive to time consuming reform. The elections of 2002 were the first four-year term mandates in post Dayton Bosnia and Herzegovina. The OHR has embarked on an aggressive campaign to eliminate corruption and bureaucratic overspending. Steps to

attract foreign investment have finally been implemented. European standards are being pushed on taxes, environment and transparency.

What this means for the ordinary person here is hope for a stable
future. The short-term reality however is a rather corrupt system that
lacks a coherent vision of building a united country. Great strides have
been made but life in Bosnia and Herzegovina still faces rough economic
times, with war criminals still not brought to justice, and many people left
to deal on a daily basis with the scars of war. This may not seem so evident
to the visitor. The quest for a normal life has in many places created a lively
atmosphere. Café's are always full of smiling faces, people walk the streets
wearing the finest of European fashions, and the warm hospitality you're
sure to find everywhere will certainly make you ask 'Why did this happen
here? This is really a great place.' Bosnians ask themselves this question
every day.

PRACTICAL INFORMATION

WHEN TO VISIT

For the two co-authors of this book it's very difficult to say when the best
time to visit would be - we both live in Bosnia now and we love it all year
round. Summer and Spring are the obvious warm seasons with plenty of
fun and sun to be had. But winter skiing and the autumn colours are equally
nice. People are always out and about in this country - it's certainly one of
the most social places we've come across - and you'll never miss the local
crowds. You've got the best of both worlds here, Alpine and Mediterranean
- enjoy them both, any time of year!

In spring, the country is at its best. So green, so many flowers. The
days are pleasantly warm and the evenings are refreshingly cool. In summer time, it is nice and warm in Sarajevo, but sometimes a little too hot
(30+ °C) in Mediterranean Herzegovina. Prices for accommodation are
generally a little higher in July and August.

If you come to Bosnia and Herzegovina only once, and you are not
into winter sports, spring and summer are the best times. But if you come
to the country regularly, or if you are into wet walks, autumn is not to be
missed. October and November are good months to avoid the crowds and
enjoy the barrage of orange, red and yellow leaves that paint the forests.
These months see both rainy and cool, sunny days.

Bosnia in general and the mountainous regions in particular have very
cold winters and high snow precipitation. If you are a skier, the best time
for a visit is from January to March. Olympic skiing on the Bjelašnica,
Igman and Jahorina mountains is perfect in these three months. In this
period, people from the region flock to these areas. If you plan on coming
and you want a hotel close to the ski lifts, it is best to make reservations.
And make sure to buy snow chains: the road clearance teams are getting
better but the roads in winter are still not quite as good as they would be
in other parts of the world.

ENTERING BOSNIA AND HERZEGOVINA

With the right papers, entering Bosnia and Herzegovina is easy. Procedures at both the borders and the airport are standardized and uncompli-

cated. Only during the holiday season, when the people living in the Diaspora flock into the country, do border crossings sometimes take a bit of time.

Bosnia and Herzegovina can only be entered with a valid passport. EU, American and Canadian citizens do not require a visa to enter the country. Most other people do need a visa, and getting one is difficult. Visas are issued by the country's diplomatic missions. Visas for private travel require an application form and a letter of intent from somebody who resides in Bosnia and Herzegovina. Business visas require an application form, an invitation from an in-country business partner and a letter of intent from the Bosnia and Herzegovina Trade Office. Visa applicants from certain countries should also provide evidence of possession of cash assets, as well as HIV test results.

Fees for visas issued by diplomatic/consular offices:

Single entry-exit visas and transit visas	31.00 KM
Multiple entry-exit visas for periods up to 90 days	57.00 KM
Multiple entry-exit visa for periods over 90 days	72.00 KM

Officially, people who enter the country on a visa need to register themselves with the police within 24 hours after their arrival in the country. Any violation of this regulation could officially entail a financial penalty or even deportation. In reality, I have frequently received visitors who required a visa to enter, I never registered any of them and none of them ever ran into any type of problem as a consequence. Similarly, you might be asked to fill in a card upon arrival in Sarajevo Airport – but at the time of writing this card was no longer being distributed.

If you enter Bosnia and Herzegovina by car, you will have to buy vehicle insurance at the border. It is an uncomplicated and fairly inexpensive affair. You do not need this insurance if you have a green card that covers Bosnia and Herzegovina (something that is not normally the case).

Both local alcoholic beverages and cigarettes are relatively cheap in Bosnia and Herzegovina, and the only money you could save would be on brand-name alcohol. You are allowed to import 200 cigarettes and 2 liters of liquor.

DIPLOMATIC MISSIONS

Bosnia and Herzegovina embassies overseas

Australia:	5 Beale Crescent, Deakin, ACT 2600 Canberra; tel: +61 2 6232 4646; fax: +61 2 6232 55 54
Austria:	Tivoligasse 54, A-1120 Wien; tel: +43 1 810 1252; fax: +43 1 811 8569
Belgium:	Rue Tenbosch 34, 1000 Bruxelles; tel: +32 2 644 2008; fax: +32 2 644 1698
Canada:	130 Albert St, Suite 805, Ottawa, Ontario K1P 5G4; tel: +1 613 236 0028; fax: +1 613 236 1139
Croatia:	Torbarova 9, Zagreb 10000; tel: +385 1 468 3761; fax: +385 1 468 3764

Denmark: Nytory 3, 1450 Copenhagen K; tel: +45 33 33 80 40;
              fax: +45 33 33 80 17
France: 174 rue de Courcelles, 75017 Paris;
              tel: +33 1 42 67 34 22; fax: +33 1 40 53 85 22
Germany: Ibsenstrasse 14, D-10439 Berlin; tel: +49 30 814 712
              10; fax: +49 30 814 712 11
Greece: Hatzikosta 3, 11521 Atena; tel: +30 210 64 11 375;
              fax: +30 210 64 23 154
Hungary: Pasareti śt 48, 1026 Budapest; tel: +36 1 212 0106;
              fax: +36 1 212 0109
Italy: Via Fabio Filzi 19, Milano; tel: +39 02 669 82 707;
              fax: +39 02 669 81 467
The Netherlands: Bezuidenhoutseweg 223, 2594 AL, The Hague;
              tel: +31 70 35 88 505; fax: +31 70 35 84 367
Norway: Bygday Alle 10, 0262 Oslo; tel: +47 22 54 09 63;
              fax: +47 22 55 27 50
Serbia and Montenegro: Milana Tankošića 8, 11 000 Belgrade;
              tel: +381 11 329 1277
Slovenia: Kalarjeva 26, 1000 Ljubljana; tel: +386 1 432 4042;
              fax: +386 1 432 2230
Spain: Calle Lagasca 24.2, Izda, 28001 Madrid;
              tel: +349 1 575 08 70; fax: +349 1 435 50 56
Switzerland: Jungfraustrasse 1, CH-3005 Bern;
              tel: +41 31 351 1051; fax: +41 31 351 1079
Sweden: Birger Jarisgaten 55/3, 11145 Stockholm;
              tel: +468 44 00 540; +468 24 98 30
Turkey: Turan Emeksiz Sokak 3, Park Siteler 9/3,
              Gaziomanpasa, Ankara; tel: +90 312 427 3602;
              fax: +90 312 427 3604
United Kingdom: 5-7 Lexan Gardens, London W8 5JJ;
              tel: +44 20 7373 0867; fax: +44 20 7373 0871
United States of America: 2109 E St NW, Washington DC 20037;
              tel: +1 202 337 1500; fax: +1 202 337 1502

Foreign embassies in Bosnia and Herzegovina

The country code is +387. All embassies are in Sarajevo. The postcode for
Sarajevo is 71000.

Austria: Džidžikovac 7; tel: 033 668 337; fax: 033 668 339
Bulgaria: Soukbunar 15; tel: 033 668 191; fax: 033 668 182
Canada: Grbavička 4/2; tel: 033 222 033, 033 447 901;
              fax: 033 222 004
China: Braće Begić 17; 033 215 102; fax: 033 215 108
Croatia: Mehmeda Spahe 16; tel: 033 444 330/1;
              fax: 033 472 434;
              Consular Section: Skenderija 17; 033 442 591;
              fax: 033 650 328

Czech Republic: Franjevačka 19; tel: 033 447 525, 033 446 966;
            fax: 033 447 526
Denmark: Splitska 9; tel: 033 665 901; fax: 033 665 902
Egypt: Nurudina Gackića 58; tel: 033 666 498;
            fax: 033 666 499
France: Mehmed-bega Kapetanovića Ljubušaka 18;
            tel: 033 668 149, 033 668 151; fax: 033 212 186
Germany: Mejtaš-Buka 11-13; tel: 033 275 000, 033 275 080;
            fax: 033 652 978, 033 443 176
Greece: Obala Maka Dizdara 1; tel: 033 213 439;
            fax: 033 203 512
Hungary: Hasana Bibera 53; tel: 033 205 302;
            fax: 033 268 930;
            Consular Section: Safet-bega Bašagića 58a
Iran: Obala Maka Dizdara 6; tel: 033 650 210;
            fax: 033 663 910
Italy: Čekaluša 39; tel: 033 203 959; fax: 033 659 368
Japan: Mula Mustafe Bašeskije 2; tel: 033 209 580;
            fax: 033 209 583
Libya: Tahtali sokak 17; tel: 033 200 621; fax: 033 663 620
Macedonia: Emerika Bluma 23; tel: 033 269 402, 033 206 004;
            fax: 033 206 004
Malaysia: Trnovska 6; tel: 033 201 578; fax: 033 667 713
Malta: Mula Mustafe Bašeskije 12; tel: 033 668 632;
            fax: 033 668 632
Netherlands: Grbavička 4, I sprat; tel: 033 223 404, 033 223 410;
            fax: 033 223 413
Norway: Ferhadija 20; tel: 033 254 000; fax: 033 666 505
Pakistan: Emerika Bluma 17; tel: 033 211 836;
            fax: 033 211 837
Palestine: Čemerlina 4; tel: 033 272 700/1; fax: 033 238 677
Poland: Dola 13; tel: 033 201 142; fax: 033 233 796
Portugal: Čobanija 12; tel: 033 200 835; fax: 033 443 117
Romania: Tahtali sokak 13-15; tel: 033 207 447;
            fax: 033 668 940
Russia: Urijan Dedina 93-95; tel: 033 668 147;
            fax: 033 668 148
Saudi Arabia: Koševo 44; tel: 033 211 861; fax: 033 212 204
Slovenia: Bentbaša 7; tel: 033 271 260; fax: 033 271 270
Spain: Čekaluša 16; tel: 033 278 560; fax: 033 278 582
Serbia and Montenegro: Obala Maka Dizdara 3a; tel: 033 260 080;
            fax: 033 221 469
Sweden: Ferhadija 20; tel: 033 276 030; fax: 033 276 060
Switzerland: Josipa Štadlera 15; tel: 033 275 850;
            fax: 033 665 246
Turkey: Hamdije Kreševljakovića 5; tel: 033 445 260;
            fax: 033 443 190

United Kingdom: Tina Ujevića 8; tel: 033 282 200;
          fax: 033 666 131;
          Consular Section: Petrakijina 11; tel: 033 208 229;
          fax: 033 204 780
United States of America: Alipašina 43; tel: 033 445 700;
          fax: 033 659 722
Vatican: Pehlivanuša 9; tel: 033 207 847; fax: 033 207 863

In Mostar

Office of United States of America: Mostarskog bataljona bb;
          tel: 036 580 580
Consulate of Republic Croatia: Zagrebačka 8; tel: 036 316 630
General Consulate of Republic Turkey: Mala Tepa 24;
          tel: 036 551 209

In Banja Luka

Austria: Jovana Dučića 52; tel: 051 311 144
Croatia: Milana Karanovića 1; tel: 051 304 258
Germany and France: DR.M.Stojanovića 1; tel: 051 303 925
United Kingdom: Simeuna Đaka 8; tel: 051 216 843
United States of America: Jovana Dučića 5; tel: 051 221 590

GETTING THERE AND AWAY

Bosnia and Herzegovina has a well-connected capital. It is easily accessible by air, bus, or train. The airport is only 20 minutes away from the city centre and has direct flights to many European capitals and thus indirect flights to everywhere else. Many local and international bus lines depart from the centre of town. The train schedule is less extensive, but does offer a few really good trips in comfortable trains at very modest prices.

By air

The state-of-the-art Sarajevo airport (033 289 100) is located at the base of Mount Igman. In winter, this is probably the worst possible location for an airport in Sarajevo and surroundings. In the cold months, early-morning flights are regularly cancelled as the entire area is often covered with heavy fog until late morning or later. In all other seasons, this airport is a pleasure to arrive at and depart from.

The airport is 12 km from the town centre. There are no shuttle buses and no bus routes in the vicinity of the airport. At various rates, the major hotels - and some of the smaller ones - offer airport pick-ups and drop-offs. Otherwise, taxis will take you to town for either the meter fee or a fixed amount of 20 KM.

You can change money at the airport exchange desk, rent a car from one of the car rental boots located in the arrival hall, and, in case you need to contact your hotel, buy a phone card at the post office. If your luggage did not arrive, you have to register the missing suitcases at the lost and found office, located next to the coffee shop in the arrival hall.

As Bosnia and Herzegovina is neither a main destination nor a major hub, flights to Sarajevo are relatively costly. The most affordable tickets used to come from the official airline of Bosnia and Herzegovina - Air Bosna – but this airline recently went bankrupt. Depending on the season, a return ticket from London will cost between £200 and £400. From most Euro countries a ticket will costs between 250 and 450 Euro, and from New York it will be between $700 and a little over $1,000. At the time of writing, ten international carriers have regular flights to and from Sarajevo:

Adria Airways: Ferhadija 23/II; tel: 033 289 245 (airport), 033 232 125/6; fax: 033 233 692

Avio Express Airlines: Zelenih beretki 22; tel: 033 653 179; fax: 033 208 334

Austrian Airlines: Maršala Tita 54; tel: 033 474 445 (airport), 033 474 446/7; fax: 033 470 526

Croatia Airlines: Kranjčevićeva 4/1a; tel: 033 258 600 (airport), 033 666 123; fax: 033 463 158

Lufthansa: Alipašina bb; tel: 033 474 445 (airport), 033 278 590/1/2

Turkish Airlines: Kulovića 5; tel: 033 289 249 (airport), 033 666 092; 033 212 938

Malev: Kurta Schorka 36; tel: 033 289 246 (airport), 033 473 200/1; fax: 033 467 105

JAT: Zelenih beretki 6; tel: 033 259 750 (airport), 033 259 750/1; fax: 033 223 083

Sometimes, it is cheaper to buy your tickets from a travel agency. The cheapest and most reliable ticket agent in Sarajevo is Kompas Travel in the city centre (Maršala Tita 8; tel: 033 208 014; fax: 033 208 015; email: kompas@kompas-sarajevo.com; web: www.kompas-sarajevo.com). A comprehensive overview of all other travel agencies is available at the Sarajevo Old Town Tourist Information Office.

There are international airports in Mostar, Tuzla and Banja Luka as well.

By ferry

Bosnia and Herzegovina has only one tiny strip of coast at Neum and there are no ferries that dock there. With seasonal schedules, ferries do come from Italy (Ancona and Bari) to the ports of Split and Dubrovnik. If you are traveling by car, these ferries may save you traffic jams along the Croatian coast. If you do not have your own means of transport, you will find the transfer to the bus stations at the port (in Split) or close to it (in Dubrovnik) easy and hassle-free. If you are a ferry person, check the ferry companies websites: SEM (www.sem-marina.hr), Jadrolinija (www.jadrolinija.hr) and Adriatica Navigazione (www.adriatica.it).

By rail

Buses drive fast, use curvy roads and confine you to your chair from beginning to end. Getting around by train is a little slower, but much more comfortable. In Bosnia and Herzegovina, trains are punctual, low-cost, and sometimes fairly luxurious, with couches that can be turned into beds, and cabins that are very often completely empty.

Before the war the rail network connected most Bosnian cities. This has changed dramatically. There are now only three routes that originate in Sarajevo: the Sarajevo-Zenica-Banja Luka-Zagreb route takes about ten hours from start to finish; the northern route to Budapest goes via Tuzla; and the southern route towards the Adriatic coast is Konjic-Jablanica-Mostar-Čapljina-Ploče (Ploče is in Croatia). This last route goes through the Neretva Canyon and is particularly scenic. Even on these three routes, trains do not go quite as frequently as the buses do.

Daily trains to and from Sarajevo

	To	From	cost (KM)	duration
Budapest	20.20	18.30	92/180	13 hours
Ploče	06.20/18.40	05.00/13.30	18/29	5 hours
Zagreb	09.49	09.00	45/74	9 hours

Recently, Bosnia and Herzegovina joined the Eurorail system. Perhaps that will fill up these sadly empty trains a bit more.

By bus

The bus system of Bosnia and Herzegovina functions well. Centrotrans and a range of smaller bus companies have reliable bus routes to and from all towns and many villages. Every city and town has a bus station with the daily departure and arrival times posted in local language on the station's wall. Ask the people behind the counters if the schedule is not clear to you: they are not likely to speak English (though in Sarajevo they often do) but will point you in the right direction. Asking a person who is standing around waiting is also a good way of double-checking that you are getting on the right bus. People are very willing to help.

Bus travel is reasonably priced and a one-way ticket to the furthest in-country destination from Sarajevo will not cost more than 30 KM. At the smaller stations, you pay when you get on the bus. At the main bus stations, you are meant to buy your ticket at the ticket booth, but even there you can normally get it on the bus as well. Usually there is an extra charge of 1 or 2 KM for each sizeable bag you carry with you. Bus stations do not have lockers or temporary luggage storage places.

Longer trips have breaks, the frequency and duration of which depending on whether or not the driver smokes. In addition, bus drivers may have special deals with restaurants en route. If so, the breaks will be longer to encourage you to eat and drink.

You might want to check out the bus before you get on. Most buses are comfortable and clean but there is the occasional company that has ratty buses with broken seats, windows that don't open, no air conditioning and a driver who smokes the entire length of the journey.

Useful terms

place of departure	mjesto odlaska
destination	destinacija
day of trip	dan vožnje (Pon-Mon, Uto-Tue, Sri-Wed, Čet-Thu, Pet-Fri, Sub-Sat, Ned-Sun)
time of departure	vrijeme odlaska
search	pretraga
departure	odlazak
arrival	dolazak
duration	trajanje
price	cijena

Centrotrans is a Eurolines member and runs regular buses from many European destinations to Sarajevo. Bus schedules, on-line reservations and main European office addresses can be found on the Centrotrans website: www.centrotrans.com. At the time of writing, the Centrotrans schedule is as follows:

From	Days	Single (KM/Euros)	Return (KM/Euros)
Amsterdam	Wed, Sat	250/127	370/188
Antwerp	Wed	230/114	330/165
Berlin	Sat	225/115	325/115
Dortmund	Mon, Tue, Thu, Fri, Sat	239/122	358/183
Dubrovnik	every day	40/20.50	60/ 30.5
Hamburg	Fri	239/122	358/183
Ljubljana	Mon, Wed, Fri	70/36	120/ 61
Makarska	every day	27/14	38/ 19.5
Munich	every day	102/52	141/ 72
Pula	Mon, Wed, Fri, Sat	80/41	130/ 66.5
Rotterdam	Sun, Thu	240/122	340/174
Stuttgart	Sun	156/80	235/120
Split	every day	30/15.50	45/ 23
Vienna	every day	72/37	115/ 59
Zagreb	every day	50/25.50	80 / 41

By car

If you are in a hurry to get from A to B, Bosnia and Herzegovina is not the ideal place to be. There are no real highways and there is not much scope for high-speed driving as roads tend to wind through river valleys and up-and downhill. However, if you are not in any particular hurry, driving from town to town in Bosnia and Herzegovina is as pleasant as driving gets. There is lots of beautiful scenery, the roads tend to be quiet, and there are plenty of quality places to stop for a drink or a meal. Strangely, some of the country's best restaurants are right next to a major road. There is little chance of running out of petrol in the middle of nowhere as there are many petrol stations pretty much everywhere. Equally comforting is the number of garages. For relatively little money and almost always right away, the 'automehaničar' will make repairs and the 'vulkanizer' will fix your flat tire.

Driving in Bosnia and Herzegovina is nice, but some warnings are in order:

- The first few times you go through them, the tunnels of Bosnia and Herzegovina are unnerving. They are unlit and entering them on a sunny day is blinding. Your eyes will need a few seconds to adjust to the pitch black. You cannot just assume that straight driving will be safe as tunnels may curve and may have pot-holes and water dripping from the ceiling. Most tunnels have a sign indicating the length of the tunnel to prepare you for what is in store. Don't forget to take off your sunglasses before entering! I forgot it once and will never forget the experience.

- Take a good map with you. Road signs in some areas are frequent and accurate but they may suddenly be gone altogether.

- Road signs in the Republika Srpska are mostly in Cyrillic. There is a Cyrillic alphabet section in the back of this book.

- First-hand and second-hand spare parts for German-made cars are widely available. For other cars, spare parts may be a little more difficult to find.

- People might tell you that fuel is best bought in the Federation, as some stations in the Republika Srpska have a reputation for mixing water in with the fuel. I have never had any trouble myself.

- The law stipulates that you always have to carry a spare tyre, a jack, an extra headlight bulb, a first-aid kit, a tow rope and a hazard triangle. During a routine police check you may have to show that you do indeed have all that.

- In the winter period, snow chains are vital.

It takes three hours to reach Sarajevo from the border at Metković/Doljani in southern Dalmatia. The route going through Trebinje and Stolac takes one hour more, but nonetheless has my personal preference every time I go to Dubrovnik, as the route is scenic and quiet. From the Split area the best route goes through Kamensko, Livno, Bugojno and Travnik. The route through Tomislav-Grad to Jablanica is stunning, but much of the road is not asphalted, and there are a few forks without signs. There is a road from Sinj via Bili Brig to Livno as well. It may look tempting on the map but is all but inaccessible in reality. From the north, the quickest route to Sarajevo is from Slavonski Brod and Bosanski Brod. However, this route is *not* advisable if this is your first trip to the country. The reason is the war damage you'll see along the road between Brod and Doboj. With every single house completely destroyed for kilometers on stretch, this is perhaps the most depressing road in the country. The routes going through Bihać or Banja Luka are longer but do not look so awful.

Renting a car is easy but costly. Daily rate vary from 75KM to 150KM (with occasional offers at lower prices), with discounts offered if you rent for a longer period. All major cities have car-rental companies. If you arrive at the Sarajevo airport you will find several rental places at the airport. F Rent a Car SA (Kranjčevićeva 39; tel: +387 33 219 177; email: fracsa@team.ba; web: www.frac.co.ba) does airport pick-ups and offers some of the best rates in town, but occasionally fails to give you the car they promised. Avis (tel: +387 33 463 598; fax: +387 33 523 030), Budget (+387 33 234 842 ext. 216), Europcar (tel: +387 33 289 273; fax: +387 33 460 737; email: asa-rent@bih.net.ba) and Hertz (tel: +387 33 668 186) all have desks at the airport. It's usually not a problem to rent a car without reservations when you arrive. Local information on many of the major car-rental companies can be found via links from the international websites and international toll-free phone numbers. Budget offers automatic transmission cars.

Hitchhiking

Unlike hitchhiking in Western Europe, hitchhiking in Bosnia and Herzegovina is not a thing for young people only. On the contrary: many hitchhikers appear to be well over 60.

In the rural areas of Bosnia and Herzegovina, hitchhiking is common practice. In and around the bigger cities it is slightly less common, but there, too, long waits are the exception. Young women rarely hitchhike alone. As in other countries: don't get in if you don't trust the driver.

By bicycle

Roads are often rather narrow and road biking is rare. With the many fast and reckless drivers, biking is not altogether safe on the main routes. But certain parts of the country are just perfect for biking. You can bike for hours on end without experiencing much traffic at all in Popovo polje from Stolac towards Trebinje, or in the large, picturesque valleys of Livanjsko and the Glamočko fields in western Bosnia.

Mountain biking is better still. Hundreds of highland villages are connected by good gravel roads almost everywhere in the country. Igman-Bjelašnica-Visočica in the Sarajevo area offers days of mountain biking trails in breathtaking mountain landscapes.

Bikers should follow the same safety precautions as hikers and stick to the roads and marked paths. Don't wander if you don't know where you are and where you are going. Roads have been cleared of mines, even the isolated gravel ones, but in some places a mine could be just 10m off the side of the road. If you don't know, don't go – or go with a guide.

Hiking

It is already obvious within town: the people from Bosnia and Herzegovina like walking. The habit of taking the car for whatever errand does not exist here, and leisure time with friends or family is often spent on foot, with long strolls through town or in the park. Municipal authorities respect this hobby, and most towns have designated areas for pedestrians only.

And they don't only stroll: all age groups hike, and the hikes they make are often so heavy that the average foreigner will be unable to keep up. These hikes are made for fun – though they can easily take you from town to town and end in family visits - and the routes chosen are beautiful. Deep canyons, raging rivers, high Dinaric peaks, endemic flowers and plants and breathtaking views wherever you turn. For good reasons, big roads are avoided. Pavements do not exist in between towns, road shoulders are rare, and drivers have little respect for pedestrians.

The former Yugoslavia had one of the best-developed systems of mountain trails in Europe. The 'transverzala' connected the Slovenian Alps with the mountains in Macedonia - these trails went through the heart of Bosnia and Herzegovina. Due to the war many trails have disappeared, but mountain associations are in the process of restoring them. The trails' marks are red circles with white dots in the middle. Seeing one is a good sign that you are on a trail that eventually leads to somewhere. You may find the marks on trees or large stones along the trail. The best marked mountain with trail maps is Bjelašnica. The mountain association sells maps and has done an excellent job of keeping the trails clearly marked.

As said repeatedly before, it is not advisable to walk or hike without first checking the mine situation. If you are on a trail that has obviously not been trekked for some time or has faded trail markings you may not want to be there. Fresh trail markings mean that the mountain associations have had the area checked and that they trek it themselves. It is wise to bring a map, compass and GPS if you have one. Check out the sections on safety and what to take for a few additional notes on hiking and hiking requirements.

If you are into hiking, you might want to buy another book of this series. 'Forgotten Beauty' by Matias Gomes describes all hikes over 2,000 meters throughout the country. Without such a book, even the most experienced hiker is recommended to go with a guide. There are literally hundreds of safe trails to trek and hike on. Best not to do it alone.

TOURIST INFORMATION

There are plans to establish a few Bosnia and Herzegovina tourist offices abroad, but at the time of writing none of them had yet opened its doors. The embassies have little or no tourist information available.

Once you are in Sarajevo, the situation is much better. There is a very good tourist information office located close to the cathedral. (tel: 033 220 721/724; fax: 033 532 281; email: tour.off@bih.net.ba; web: www.sarajevo-tourism.com; stand with your back to the cathedral and walk straight down the walkway past Central Café; turn left on Zelene beretke and look for number 22a, 50m down on the right-hand side). Information on hotels, museums, excursions, city tours and other activities is all readily available, and their maps and leaflets are for free. The staff speak English, German,

French and Turkish. They appear to enjoy their work and will go out of their way to help. The very same people give superb guided tours through town.

Alternatively, you could simply check www.city.ba, an up-to-date website on events in the city. The International Women's Club of Sarajevo has produced a well-made practical 'mini' guide to Sarajevo called Opening Doors to Sarajevo, a Selected Guide. The guide is worth the 10KM it costs. Part of the money goes to a good cause.

There is a reasonable tourism information office close to the old bridge in Mostar as well (tel: 036 580 833; email: info@touristinfomostar.co.ba; web: www.touristinfomostar.co.ba).

MAPS

Good road maps of Bosnia and Herzegovina are available in most travel shops, bookshops and airports around Europe. Due to Croatia's odd shape, most maps of Croatia include all of Bosnia and Herzegovina. In-country, maps can be found at a few petrol stations and in some of the bookshops.

All updated European maps include Bosnia and Herzegovina and its main communication arteries. They lack detail and will make you lose your way. The routes suggested by web-based route finders are OK, but the maps are too vague and the estimated travel times do not make any sense at all as the route finders assume unrealistically high average speeds.

The Freytag and Berndt map of Bosnia and Herzegovina and Europe (1:250,000), the Studio FMB map (1:300,000) and the Trasat Polo map of Bosnia and Herzegovina, Croatia and Slovenia (1:500,000) are all good and cost in the range of 12-16 KM. Maps can also be found at www.kakarigi.net/maps (hundreds of maps of cities, towns, mountains and lakes but no map of the country as a whole), www.mapabih.com (for business people) and www.embassyworld.com/maps (lots of links to all sorts of maps). The maps that are available, free of charge, from tourism information centers around the country show the main routes only. If you are really, really into maps, you might want to buy Povijesni Atlas Bosne i Hercegovine, a book with 350 pages of historic maps. At the time of writing, it exists in the local language only, but there are plans to translate it into English.

HEALTH

The chance of getting one of the standard travelers' diseases is very slight, as drinking water throughout the country is excellent and food hygiene is good. Bosnia and Herzegovina has no legal requirements for vaccinations, but visitors are generally advised to be immunized against hepatitis A and B, tetanus, diphtheria, polio, and typhoid. Note that many people ignore this, and that I have never heard of anybody getting sick as a consequence.

To find a pharmacy, ask for 'apoteka'. In major centers, there are many of them, and there is usually at least one that is open 24 hours a day. These pharmacies will generally have all regular prescription drugs readily available. In villages and smaller towns, you may not find a pharmacy at all. If you do find one, it may not stock what you need. The best pharmacy in the country is probably Sarajevo Pharmacy at Saliha Hadžihuseinovića

Muvekita 11 in Sarajevo (tel: 033 722 666; fax: 033 722 667; email: apoteke@bih.net.ba; web: www.apoteke-sarajevo.com).

Public health clinics in Bosnia and Herzegovina are not what they should be, but there are some very good doctors in most towns. It is best to contact your embassy if you need medical attention, as embassies usually have lists of doctors they have good experiences with.

SAFETY

You are going to Bosnia? Are you sure? Why would you do that? Is it safe there? Aren't there mines?

You can't come to Bosnia and Herzegovina without having this conversation. It is an understandable concern: there *are* mines in Bosnia and Herzegovina and, with the clearing process progressing slowly, there will continue to be mines for the decades to come. But that does not mean that visiting Bosnia and Herzegovina is unsafe. So far, no visitor to Bosnia and Herzegovina has ever been involved in a mine incident.

Mine safety is a matter of respecting a few rules:

- Highly populated areas, national parks and conservation areas are all clear of mines and safe to visit.
- Stay away from taped areas. Whether in yellow or red, whether the markings are new or old: just simply never go there.
- If you are in the countryside, stay away from areas that are not obviously frequented by people. Look for cut grass, tire tracks, footprints or rubbish – all indications of safe areas. Obviously, areas in which people are walking, jogging, BBQ-ing et cetera are safe. Conversely, abandoned villages – however much fun it seems to explore them - may pose a threat.
- The most dangerous areas are the former lines of confrontation in the countryside. Many mountain ranges and some rural areas are still contaminated. As tourists and travelers would not normally know much about the location of these former confrontation lines, it is best to take a guide or a local who knows the terrain. Mountain associations and eco-tourism organizations are your best bet for a safe mountain adventure. There is plenty of safe hiking, walking, wandering and exploring to be done in Bosnia and Herzegovina – it is simply not wise to do it alone.

For more information, you could visit the Mine Action Centre (MAC; Zmaja od Bosne 8 in Sarajevo) or visit the center's website (www.bhmac.org).

Apart from the mines, Bosnia and Herzegovina is one of the safest places in Europe. Violent crime is virtually non-existent. For men and women alike, walking the streets of any town or city at any time of day or night is a relatively safe bet.

Traffic may be risky. Most of Bosnia and Herzegovina's roads are narrow and curvy. Road maintenance is getting better but don't let a pot-hole surprise you. The locals tend to drive fast and have little fear of overtaking on a solid line. Other than that, the main concerns for travelers are car thieves and pickpockets. Always lock your car doors, and engage your alarm if you have one. In trams and buses, keep your purse closed and your wallet in your front pocket. Pickpockets are quick and talented, and you will not even know that you have been had until later. They usually work in pairs.

Mountain safety

Bringing a few extras on your hikes adds weight but could save your life in an emergency situation. It is always good to bring high-energy food items. Even outside the summer months a hat and 15+ sunscreen are essential in the mountains. The high mountain sun exposure can be particularly dangerous in summer and a sunstroke is a bad thing to get when you are hours away from help. To prevent sunstroke, also protect your face and back of the neck when the sun is particularly fierce.

Bring water, but also try the sources you'll find on your way. Most water sources are perfectly safe for drinking. Stay away if a source is clogged with moss and algae. Mountain huts on spots without sources closeby generally have water storage reservoirs. If you come across a metal lid near a hut it is probably a rain collection tank. Check it first, but they are usually good for drinking.

Bosnia and Herzegovina is a mountainous land and each valley and range has its own unique system. A rainy day in town could coincide with a sunny afternoon on the mountains around it and freezing winds on their peaks. A consequence is that the weather conditions in town should not affect your packing. The high altitude mountain ranges can experience drastic temperature changes. When a storm or fog rolls in, the temperature can easily drop 10-15° C in a matter of hours. Consequently, even if it is pleasantly warm in town, a warm fleece and an extra shirt and socks could help prevent catching a cold in the mountains.

Many trails are not as well-maintained as they were before the war, so it is best to wear good boots that give you adequate ankle support. Loose rocks, fallen tree limbs or erosion can be enough to twist an ankle and abruptly end your hike.

There are two types of poisonous snakes in Bosnia and Herzegovina. Although their bites are rarely fatal, your first aid box should contain a snake bite kit. These kits can be purchased in most outdoor shops in the West. They are compact, easy to carry, and normally come with very clear instructions. Prevention, of course, is the best protection. Be aware of where you are stepping. In the summer months snakes can be found in clear water rivers and streams. They will also gather on the sunny side of mountains. Be careful around rocky areas with cracks and holes; these are snakes' favorite hiding spots. In the early autumn they tend to linger on tree limbs. The colder air makes them rather lethargic and they are less of a threat than during the hot season. Poisonous snakes only inject venom 25% of the time. If you are bitten it is best to stay calm. The faster your blood circulates the faster the poison travels through your system. Don't let this information scare you. Snakes are more afraid of you than you are of them, and anxious to get out of your way.

Lightning strikes occur frequently on high ridges during a storm, particularly above river canyons. If you see lightning while you are trekking on a ridge get out of there quickly. There are often signs (such as struck-down black pines) that indicate you're in a dangerous area.

It is good practice to let someone know if you plan to hike solo. If you are going with a guide, safety precautions have probably been taken – but it might be wise to check. A mountain rescue service (Gorska služba za spašavanje - GSS) exists but is not present in every region. Rescuers do not always have access to helicopter assistance and it may take some time to reach you in case of an emergency.

WHAT TO TAKE

Almost anything can be bought in Bosnia and Herzegovina, and most items are relatively inexpensive.

In addition to the usual, you might want to take:

- An international driving license if you are not from the surrounding or EU countries.
- Adapters for UK or American plugs. These adapters are not for sale in Bosnia and Herzegovina. The country uses the standard European size and shape (220V and 50Hz) with twin round-pin plugs.
- Sunglasses. Summers are bright, spring and autumn have plenty of bright days, and the reflection of the sun off the snow in winter is blinding.
- A light pair of slippers if you plan on staying with Bosnians or in private accommodation. Most homes have extra slippers, called papuče, but I always find it nice to have my own.
- A jumper. Spring and autumn are similar in that many days are warm and sunny but evenings are chilly. The air is very refreshing but not if you're not dressed adequately. Even on the hottest days in the summer, evenings can be cool.
- The right footwear. The beaches are rocky and full of pebbles, walks require comfortable walking shoes or more, and even in the midst of town many pavements are covered with ice and dirty, cold slush in winter.
- Good winter gear. Thermal underwear, gloves, hat, scarf and rain gear are recommended.

If you intend to hike, you should not forget:

- A water bottle, to be filled at the many springs that you'll pass by on your walks.
- A sunhat, especially if you are planning to do high mountain hikes.
- A snake-bite suction kit, as it's better to be safe than sorry.
- Very sturdy mountain shoes or boots, as many of the trails are not well maintained and loose rocks or roots could cause a serious ankle injury.
- A warm fleece, light rain gear, walking sticks if you use them, and a comfortable rucksack.

- Camping gear, although some of the campsites in Bosnia and Herzegovina provide tents, mats and even sleeping bags.
- Good waterproof gear (gaiters, poncho, waterproof trousers, a protective coat on your shoes) is a good idea if you visit the country in any season other than mid-summer.

Two warnings:
- Winter hiking in this country is an amazing experience, but be prepared for more than 1m of snow above the 1,000m mark during the coldest months. Bring whatever waterproof gear you have. Warm fleeces and thermals are a must. If you plan to hike to over 2,000m, boots that can be worn with crampons are best. If you don't have such gear, you could rent it from a local eco-tourism operator.
- Many travelers find it cool to dress down. Bosnia and Herzegovina is not the country for that. People tend to dress casually, even in fancy places, but their casual clothing matches and is clean and refined. In general, people attach importance to appearance

MEDIA

In the war years, television and radio stations functioned as propaganda machines. There were three main stations, each with limited reach. In addition, there were many dozens of small broadcasters, often focusing on not more than a single municipality. A few years ago, each of these stations was scrutinized and many were closed down. Although many small broadcasters still exist, if only for a few hours per week, most people in Bosnia and Herzegovina have by now moved to one of the larger stations.

There are three main television stations. Luckily for foreign viewers, none of them dubs English language programs. The Federation television station (FTV) and its Republika Srpska counterpart (RTRS) are the two stations envisioned by the Dayton Peace Agreement. They air foreign movies, news, documentaries, music specials and soaps. The best independent station is the Sarajevo-based Hayat. On air 24 hours a day for the people in Bosnia and Herzegovina and for the large diaspora in Europe and North America, Hayat broadcasts local and foreign movies and series, local news, talk shows and documentaries from all over the world. Hayat produces programs as well, for its own use and, on occasion, for CNN. Refreshingly, Hayat does not limit itself to bad news, and managed to give Bosnia and Herzegovina a bit of positive coverage through CNN.

Bosnia Daily is the only English language newspaper in Bosnia and Herzegovina. It is available by electronic subscription only (www.bosniadaily.co.ba; bdaily@megatel.ba). Most subscribers are members of the international community in Bosnia and Herzegovina, and the daily's very strong focus on the role and activities of the international community is therefore logical - but nonetheless somewhat annoying for the outsider. Other than that, this is a relatively good newspaper that carries interesting articles in surprisingly good English.

Apart from Bosnia Daily, all newspapers and magazines are printed in the local language. Perhaps more than anywhere else in the world, the written press feels that bad news sells better than good news, and tends to look very critically at whatever they see around. Endless training from the British and the Americans – through BBC and IREX – have not changed the media's inclination to criticize anything and everything. Going through the local language newspapers, one gets the wrong impression that there is no progress and no hope of progress in this country.

COMMUNICATIONS

Post

Letters to a home address tend to arrive but may take a long time. Packages are a bit riskier and collecting them can be time-consuming. You will receive a yellow slip at the place you are staying, indicating a period within which you should collect your package. With this yellow slip and an ID, you have to come to the post office and go through quite some form-filling and fee-paying. Do not be surprised if your package looks opened and tattered.

There appears to be no service standards and the post office experience depends entirely on the individuals behind the counter. It happened that I walked into a post office, bought stamps and telephone cards, sent a letter by registered mail, and was done within a few minutes. On another occasion, I found the post office staff in the midst of their coffees and cigarettes, seemingly unaware of the people waiting at the counter. Eventually they looked up and started to help people in random order (the discretion line meant nothing to most customers), charging dubious fees in the process.

Telephone

Phoning to Bosnia and Herzegovina: **+387**

Phoning from Bosnia and Herzegovina: **00** – country code – city code without the **0** - number.

Phoning from hotels is often senselessly expensive. Check the prices before you chat away. Phone booths – you will find them at the bus stations and post offices – are a lot cheaper, but still charge more than what you are probably used to. The phones do not accept coins. 10 KM and 20 KM cards can be bought from the post office or at the small newspaper kiosks. Beware: different phone companies provide their services in different parts of the country and your phone cards may not be valid once you leave the town you bought them in.

The companies charge different fees and their nationalist agendas shine through these fees. From Sarajevo, a phone call to Belgrade will cost you quite a bit. Conversely, a call to Belgrade from Banja Luka is considered a local call, and there is no need to even dial the country code. If you intend to make long phone calls, you might even want to cross the entity line if that is only a bus stop away from where you are. In all cases, it is cheaper to phone after 19.00.

Mobile phones have taken Bosnia and Herzegovina by storm. Currently, there are three GSM servers in the country: BiH telecom (061), Eronet (063) and Mobi (065). Unlike the phone card systems, the signals of these servers overlap. This means that, unless you are in the midst of nature or in an isolated village, the signal is generally good.

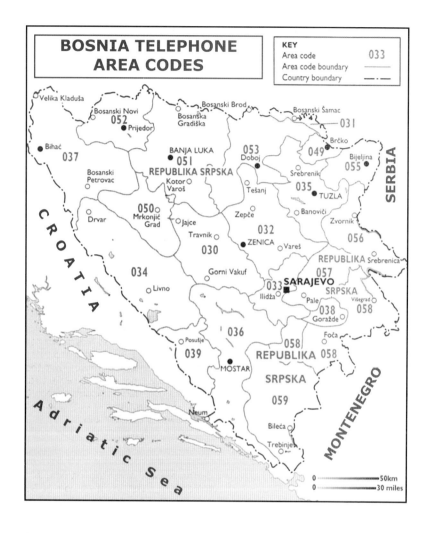

European GSM mobiles have roaming agreements with Bosnia and Herzegovina, but roaming prices are high. American and Canadian mobile phones do not allow for roaming at all. In either case, you might want to buy a local SIM card. The first purchase of a local SIM ultra card costs 50 KM, including 10 KM call credit. Call credit is available in the form of 20 KM and 50 KM cards, and can be bought from the post office or at the small newspaper kiosks.

Telephone numbers

Emergencies	124
Police	122
Fire	123
Ambulance	124
Emergency roadside service	1282, 1288
Telegram service	1202
Express delivery (EMS)	1417
Operator, local numbers	1182, 1185, 1186, 1188
Operator, international numbers	1201

Internet

Bosnia and Herzegovina does not have the quick, fluid internet communication that is now common in the West, and has just started to scratch the surface of cyber culture. An increasing number of businesses, including hotels and tourist attractions, have websites and email addresses, but the information content is often limited and emails are not always replied to. Since 2001, internet cafes have been popping up. They typically charge 1 KM per hour and the connections are usually slow. In the main towns, many hotels offer internet connections as well, at various fees.

MONEY

Originally, the KM was pegged to the German mark. With the introduction of the Euro, the KM changed its peg without the least bit of trouble (1.95 KM for 1 Euro). Most shops will accept payment in Euro bills, using a 1 to 2 ratio. There are many ATM machines in all major towns and cities.

US dollars, British pounds, Yens and other major currencies can be exchanged at the banks and exchange offices that are present in most major towns. They also swap your leftover KMs back into any of these main currencies. Most banks do not have a fixed fee, but take a percentage of the total amount. As this percentage varies, you should do a bit of research before exchanging large amounts of money. Travelers' cheques are unusual, and appear to be taken by the Central Profit Bank in the old town of Sarajevo only.

Although credit cards are increasingly widely accepted in major towns, you should not rely on them. Even in the bigger towns almost nobody accepts American Express.

Make sure you have all the cash you need before leaving the major towns, as it is next to impossible to find a money machine or anybody who accepts credit card payments in smaller towns and villages.

In case of emergency: Raiffeisen Bank handles Western Union money transfers.

Normalizing life in Bosnia and Herzegovina

People sometimes get frustrated because, almost a decade after the end of the war, the standard of living is still far below what it was in pre-war Yugoslavia. But there *is* obvious progress in many fields. Take money. In the early post-war period, different parts of the country used to have different currencies. Today, the 'Convertible Mark' (KM or BAM) is fully trusted, experiences little or no inflation, and is accepted anywhere in the country.

BUDGETING

This country is not quite as cheap as the 10 dollar-a-day destinations in the developing world, but if you are used to Western Europe and North America, you will find Bosnia and Herzegovina surprisingly inexpensive. Food, going out, transport: it all costs very little and the prices get even lower when you leave the urban centres.

Most food in Bosnia and Herzegovina is of high quality and very affordable. A fine three-course meal in a good restaurant will cost some 20 to 30 KM, excluding modestly priced beverages. If you have much less to spend it is possible to have a 3 KM meal with pies and yoghurt or to get affordable food from any of the many supermarkets.

Going out is possible whatever your budget. If you have little, do as many Bosnians do: stroll, drink espressos for 1 KM and eat ice cream for 0.5 KM. If you have a little more, a world of possibilities opens up. Cinemas cost 5 KM and theatre tickets set you back between 5 and 25 KM. Discotheques ask relatively high prices (3 to 5 KM) for their drinks but do not usually charge an entry fee.

Transport between cities is very reasonably priced. Mostar to Sarajevo will cost you between 10 and 18 KM, for example. Within town, buses are always cheap, but taxi prices depend on the town you're in. The general rule appears to be: the smaller the town and the lower the number of taxis, the more expensive they are.

In comparison, accommodation seems a little overpriced. Most hotels will not accommodate you for less than 60 KM per night in a single, or less than 75 in a double. If you are a budget traveler, you should not stay in such hotels. Instead, you should pay anything between 15 and 25 KM per night for a bed in a private house. That cuts back costs significantly. If you then spend most days enjoying the city's lively streets and parks, not its restaurants and organized tours and trips, Bosnia and Herzegovina should not cost you more than 40 KM (20 euro) per day.

For hikers and adventure-seekers, day trips cost between 20 and 75 KM. A weekend trip with food, guide, transport and accommodation will cost around 150-200 KM. Week-long trips in the mountains are 700-1,200 KM, fully inclusive.

ACCOMMODATION

Hotels

The war destroyed many of the country's hotels, and in the post-war years many of the remaining hotels housed displaced people rather than tourists. But many new hotels have been built recently and many old ones have been reconstructed or renovated.

The number of stars won't tell you much. First, the categories in the Federation and the Republika Srpska are not the same, and two three-star hotels can be worlds apart. Second, the rating does not consider either the cleanliness or the hotel's atmosphere. To avoid ending up in an uncomfortable pre-war state-owned hotel, it is always wise to check out the hotel before booking in.

The main cities generally have one or more nice and fairly large hotels. Elsewhere, hotels and motels are smaller and usually family-owned. They tend to be affordable and well-kept, and you might be able to bargain a little. Most places include breakfast in the price. Breakfast might be continental or even English in the larger hotels but you are more likely to be served a thin omelet and cheese and jams with bread. Hotels usually offer half board (polu - pansion, with breakfast and dinner) or full board (pun pansion, with breakfast, lunch and dinner), but the price on the price list usually includes breakfast only. Dining out in Bosnia and Herzegovina costs so little that it may both be cheaper and more enjoyable to try out some of the restaurants in town.

There is a 2KM accommodation tax that is not usually included in the price.

Private rooms/apartments

Private accommodation is not as well-organized as in neighboring Croatia but many travel agencies in towns throughout the country do offer accommodation in apartments and private homes. Hosts are invariably friendly, but do not always speak English. A few German words are usually helpful.

In the countryside, you are unlikely to find a room sign or anything else offering private accommodation. But the locals are extremely friendly and it is not offensive to ask somebody for the possibilities. They will probably refuse money but leaving 10KM for coffee and cigarettes is a welcome gesture. Solo women travelers planning to stay in private accommodation should make sure there are other women around.

Campsites

There are quite a few campsites in Bosnia and Herzegovina. Some are close to town, but most are hard to get to and from if you don't have your own transport. Quite a few have a snack bar and toilets only, and cater mostly to day trippers. The best camping opportunities are hard to find, but can be booked through the rafting operators on the Tara, Neretva and Una rivers. It is possible to camp even if you didn't bring either a tent or mats, as some campsites pitch and equip a few tents in the summer period.

Pitching a tent on your own is possible but could be risky if you are not fully confident that you are in a mine-free area.

Mountain lodges

Unfortunately, many of the mountain lodges were destroyed during the war. But some have survived and some others have been reconstructed in the past few years. They have dormitories and a great location, and sometimes offer food. They do not normally have any single or double rooms.

EATING

From whatever angle you look at it: the people in Bosnia and Herzegovina take eating and drinking very seriously. Meals for guests are elaborate and everything is made from scratch. The number of coffee shops, bars, terraces, snack bars and restaurants around the country is mind-blowing. Picnicking families roast their lambs in their entirety. Workers generally receive a 7 to 10 KM 'hot meal allowance' per working day, meant to cover lunch but in reality often a quarter or more of their total remuneration.

Bosnia and Herzegovina's culinary traditions are very strong, and people do not like change. If what you are looking for is not within the tradition of the region, you will have difficulty finding it. The only places that might serve a typical English breakfast are the larger hotels. Pizza has been embraced (if occasionally with mayonnaise), but the Chinese, Indian and Mexican restaurants largely depend on foreigners. If you end up cooking for local people – excluding the people working for one of the international organizations – the chances they'll genuinely enjoy your food are slim.

It's best to go local. Bakeries open early and sell hot rolls, croissants, brown bread and apple and cherry strudels. You can take your breakfast to a café and enjoy it with your morning coffee. Most bakeries will make you a sandwich upon request: white bread with thick slices of cheese and bright pink processed meat with a lot of mayonnaise, generally. A little heavy for breakfast but a must-try for lunch are the famous dishes of burek, zeljanica, sirnica and krompiruša. As everything else, these filo-dough wrapped pies are made from scratch and have been a traditional meal since Ottoman times. Burek is a meat pie. Zeljanica is made from spinach and cheese. Sirnica is made from a fresh, home-made cheese and krompiruša is filo-dough with diced potatoes and spices. They may ask if you like pavlaka spread on top. Pavlaka is a fresh cream that tastes wonderful with the pita. Alternatively, try yoghurt alongside your pita. If you are into local cuisine, ask if you can watch them making these pies: it's amazing how they stretch that dough!

Dinner has more options than breakfast or lunch. The following lists include the most common dishes. Be forewarned that most people in Bosnia and Herzegovina smoke and that non-smoking restaurants do not exist.

Meats

People like eating meat

Soon after my first arrival in Bosnia and Herzegovina, I organized a workshop in a large mountain hut near Zenica. The prices were modest, the rooms looked good, and the food, the man assured me, was excellent. I ordered lunch and dinner for 25

> people. At 13.00, we got five types of meat and fries. At 19.00, we got six types of meat, fries and a small salad. When I expressed my surprise, my colleagues all assured me that these meals were exactly as meals should be.

If you like meat, you will like Bosnia and Herzegovina. Meat is a standard for any meal. With the exception of chicken, most meat is fresh from the mountainside. It is common practice here to raise all animals free range, with plenty of space and without any hormones or chemicals. You will taste the difference.

Bamija	- okra with veal.
Begova čorba	- the most popular soup, made of veal and vegetables.
Bosanski lonac	- meat stew cooked over an open fire.
Ćevapi	- small meat sausages of lamb and beef mix. They are usually served with fresh onions and pita bread on the side.
Filovane paprike	- fried peppers stuffed with minced meat and spices.
Ispod saća	- similar to a Dutch oven. A metal dish is placed on hot coals, the food is placed in the dish and covered by a lid which is then completely covered in hot coals and left to bake.
Janjetina	- lamb grilled over an open fire.
Musaka	- a meat pie made of minced beef, very similar to shepherd's pie.
Pršut	- air-dried ham, similar to Italian prosciutto.
Sarme	- meat and rice rolled in cabbage or grape leaves.
Sogandolma	- fried onions stuffed with minced meat.
Sudžuk	- beef sausages similar to pepperoni.
Suho meso	- dried beef.
Slanina	- dried bacon-like pork.
Teletina	- veal, usually served in cutlets. Veal in Bosnia and Herzegovina is not produced by locking calves in a cage to ensure softer meat.

Cheeses

Iz mjeha - sheep's milk poured into a specially sewn sheepskin 'bag.' After a time the dry cheese is taken out of the skin container and the result is a strong, dry cheese that resembles parmesan.

Kajmak - the most difficult of all cheeses to translate. It is the top layer skimmed from milk, creamy and extremely tasty. Kajmak and uštipak (doughnut-type roll) is a wonderful appetiser.

Livanjski - similar to the dry yellow cheeses of Dalmatia. It is very tasty and usually more expensive than other types of cheese. It originates from the west Bosnian town of Livno.

Mladi sir - literally means young cheese. There isn't an equivalent to it in English. It has a soft texture and is unsalted. Often it is served with a cream sauce on top. It is very healthy.

Travnički - a white, feta-like cheese from the Travnik district in central Bosnia. It is a bit salty and very popular with 'meza', which is the tradition of slow drinking and eating throughout the course of a whole day.

Vlašićki - similar to travnički cheese. It is a highland cheese from the mountain villages on Vlašić Mountain in central Bosnia.

Sweets

Baklava   - cake made with pastry sheets, nuts and sugar syrup.

Hurmašica   - date-shaped pastry soaked in a very sweet syrup sauce.

Rahatlokum   - Turkish delight, a jelly-like candy covered in powdered sugar and often served with Turkish coffee.

Ružica   - similar to baklava but baked with raisins in small roll.

Tufahija   - stewed apples stuffed with a walnut filling.

DRINKING

Water

Tourism promotion requires simple images. Bosnia and Herzegovina's first countrywide promotional brochure used the country's ancient tombstones. They are old, unique to the country and quite beautiful. Discussing the importance of national symbols at the Sarajevo University, one of the students said she didn't think the tombstone was a very appealing symbol, as the tombstone is linked with death. She suggested using the opposite - life - for future promotion material. She suggested using the country's abundant natural springs.

The student had a point. Pretty much everywhere around the country, water just comes straight out of the ground or the mountainside. Many local water supply systems are not more than a few pipes connected to one of those springs. Almost every town has one of more public fountains – often to be found in front of the mosque – and the water is invariably excellent. There are roadside fountains as well, built long ago for travelers, and most mountain walks will pass by small springs and streams of sparkling fresh water. In short, you have no worries when drinking the water in Bosnia from the tap or elsewhere. It is probably higher quality water than you have at home!

'Mineralna voda' is bottled throughout the country. Try Ilidžanski dijamant, Sarajevski kiseljak, Tešanjski dijamant or Oaza.

Coffee and tea

When in Rome, do as the Romans do. In Bosnia and Herzegovina, they drink coffee. It is the backbone of social life. During the war, when everything was scarce, coffee was amongst the most sought after commodities.

Immediately after the war ended, coffee was the main symbol of a post-war reconciliation campaign. "Tolerance. Let's have a coffee".

Nowadays, coffee is widely available and affordable. The traditional coffee is 'bosanska kafa'. It is similar to what the rest of the world calls Turkish coffee, and it is served with oddly-shaped sugar cubes and 'rahatlokum' (Turkish delight). By now, espresso and white coffee are available everywhere in towns and cities. In town, an espresso will cost you 1 KM. The other coffees are more expensive. In villages, you may well get your Bosanska kafa for 0.5 KM.

There is a tea drinking tradition as well. You'll enjoy your tea most if you drink what the locals drink. Don't ask for black tea with milk. People here don't drink it, don't know about it and don't serve it well. Try the herbal teas instead. There are a great many types and they generally have a very nice fragrance. They are often organic and come straight from the forest.

Juices

In most places, lemonade and orange juice are the only fresh squeezed juices available. Bottled juices, however, come in all sorts. The locally produced brands – *Swity* being the largest one - are wonderfully delicious. Historically, Croatia and Slovenia produced and sold the final consumer goods, while Bosnia and Herzegovina had specialized in raw commodities and half fabricates. They didn't sell directly to consumers and, consequently, they don't know *how* to sell. The result in the fruit juice sector is that Slovenian and Croatian brands dominate the market, and that the various local brands are still struggling to get the substantial market shares their products deserve. Enough of the economics though, buy local goods – it's good for the country and it's good for you!

Beer

Local beer is cheap. The first word learned by many foreign visitors is pivo. If you like beer, this word is crucial to your trip. A half-liter bottle costs 1 KM in the shop and only 2 or 3 KM in restaurants and bars. Try *Sarajevsko*, *Nektar* and *Preminger*. *Ožujsko* is a good Croatian beer that is also produced locally. In some parts of the Republika Srpska you can find Nikšičko pivo from Montenegro – it's a great beer and according to many locals one of the best in the region. Other imports are available everywhere. They are reasonably priced, but of course more expensive than local beers without really tasting any better.

Wine

The lack of advanced marketing skills shows in the wine sector as it does in the fruit juice sector. The wine-making tradition of Herzegovina dates back to Roman times, and in terms of price and quality the savory reds and dry whites of Herzegovina easily deserve a share in the world wine market. In reality, Herzegovinan wines are rarely seen outside the region. While you're in the country, try them. Stankela, Gangaš žilavka and a range of other sorts will cost you 5 to 20 KM in the shop and 15-35 KM in restaurants.

Spirits

Made from plums, pears, apples or grapes, the local spirits are amazing. They are strong, very strong, with alcohol levels commonly exceeding 40 percent. They are drunk at all times of the day and at all times of the year. Šljivovica (plum) or kruška (pear) are found more in Bosnia. Loza, made of grapes, is the specialty of Herzegovina and Dalmatia (which share the same climate and topsoil and therefore produce very similar grapes). There are a few brand names that you will find everywhere, but the best spirits are home-made. The careful process of making spirits is a male-dominated skill. The Croats in Herzegovina make the best wine and loza, the Serbs make the best šljivovica and kruška. The men who are into producing it will offer a taste of their products as if it were coffee – but with a lot more pride.

PUBLIC HOLIDAYS

Changing every year	Bajrams (Muslim Holy Days)
January 1	New Year
January 7	Orthodox Christmas
January 14	Orthodox New Year
March 1	Independence day
May 1	Labor Day
November 25	Day of the State
December 25	Catholic Christmas

SHOPPING

If you are in any of the main towns, there is a good chance you are close to a 24-hour bakery that took its fresh bread out of the oven just now. The closest grocery shop is probably less than a few minutes away. It is open from the early morning to the late evening, and quite possibly all through the night as well. It sells the exact same products as a thousand other grocery shops around the city. If you need products they do not have, you will succeed in one of the hypermarkets. Snack stands and newspaper kiosks are just around the corner, down town is for fashion and souvenirs, and everything else is spread around the city. There really isn't a thing you can't buy here, and items that are covered separately in guide books to many developing countries (film, sanitary napkins, sun lotion) are all widely available.

Prices in Bosnia and Herzegovina are fixed. While you might successfully try to reduce the price for a room in a family-owned hotel, you would look silly negotiating in Mercator or at the hair dresser. Souvenirs are the exception. When buying souvenirs, you need to bargain a little. Gently though: with rare exceptions, people are not inclined to rip you off at all. Similarly, somebody offering you coffee is not somebody trying to pull off a sales trick: it's what people *do* here.

Certainly unique to the country and the period are the war-related souvenirs. Mortars and bullets are carved and turned into anything from umbrella and candle holders to key chains and pens. Although very contemporary, these war souvenirs are carved in the same Ottoman tradition as the plates and tea and coffee sets. Made of gold, silver, copper, and bronze, all these metal works are good value for money. And they are not merely souvenirs for tourist consumption: unless you buy a plate saying 'best wishes from Bosnia and Herzegovina', you buy something that many Bosnians have at display in their homes. Similarly, the oriental-style rugs and all sorts of woodworks are no pseudo-historical tourist traps, but things that survived the centuries and are still part and parcel of Bosnian life.

INTERACTING WITH LOCAL PEOPLE

Even though there hasn't been a tourist boom since the end of the conflict, the locals are more than familiar with guests from every country in Europe and North America. Ever since the war began in 1992, tens of thousands of people came here as aid workers, soldiers, curious visitors, peace activists, diplomats, businessmen and pilgrims paying homage to the Virgin Mary in Međugorje. Consequently, you will be no surprise to the locals. The locals in the rural areas may stare a bit at first but that seems the thing to do in any small town or village in any other country that I've visited as well. You'll hardly be noticed in places like Sarajevo, Mostar or Banja Luka, where there is a significant international presence.

Local people will almost always be very friendly. This is common to the region but Bosnian hospitality is something special. Bosnians will go out of their way to assist you in finding something and often invite someone to their home for a coffee. Once you enter someone's home as a guest, expect the red carpet treatment. Rich or poor, your host will most certainly serve you coffee, followed by an offer of cigarettes. The unwritten rule is never to light up without offering the people around you a cigarette as well. More than likely the host will bring out sweets (biscuits or chocolate) and if the energy is right out comes the local spirits and food. Coming from the west, one might see it as going a bit overboard, but the tradition of treating guests like one of their own is taken seriously. My advice is to sit back and enjoy, and if you're in a rush – too bad. The best way to turn down the ninth or tenth coffee, or a chunk of meat for the vegetarian (many villagers don't understand the concept) is to say 'ne mogu', which means 'I can't.' Saying 'no, thank you' simply does not work. If you find yourself shaking from the strong Turkish coffees and just want the host to stop filling your cup then leave a bit of coffee in it. As soon as you finish the host will first give you a refill and then ask if you would like some more.

Most young people will speak at least a little bit of English, as it is taught in all the schools from an early age. American movies are popular here and many people have learned English from watching films. In western Herzegovina and northern Bosnia many people speak German. Over 300,000 refugees lived in Germany during the war and many more lived and worked in Germany before the conflict began.

For the most part, young people here don't want to speak about the war or politics. They would rather hear about new music, cool movies, good books or just shoot the breeze with you. The older generation often brings the war and politics into conversation. Many find it therapeutic so lending an ear may be the best service you can offer someone. Comments aren't even necessary. Everyone here bears a burden from the war and oftentimes they cannot handle dealing with someone else's despair. Being a good listener can have a greater effect than one can imagine.

It's nice to exchange addresses, emails, and phone numbers with people. A postcard or phone call when you get home is always much appreciated.

A few rules

People in Bosnia and Herzegovina are very tolerant. It is not easy to offend them, and the warnings that do apply are all in line with common sense.

- People have different ways of dealing with the war. Many prefer not to talk about it. Respect that.

- Begging is one of the very worst forms of child labour. If you give in to it, you encourage it. If you do not give in to it, these poor children may have to continue begging until late at night to ensure a meal or to avoid a beating. It's a dilemma. You might want to consider giving something edible (but no sweets, as these children's nutritional status is generally awful, with a deficit in everything except for sugar).

- In summer especially, the forests get very dry and there are lots of forest fires. Be very cautious.

- Dress whichever way you like, but make sure you are covered when entering a place of worship. Mosques generally have headscarves available at the entrance.

- Ask before you take photographs – refusals are rare. If you promise to send somebody a copy, send that person that copy.

- People are likely to treat you as a guest. Consequently, they would be inclined to pay for you. Remember that most people you will meet have less money than you have. If you want to pay, act quickly and be persistent, or you will fail.

- Tips are optional. Remember that people in the catering business do not normally earn a lot. On the other hand, tips are not really all that common.

Superstitions

Some Bosnians might tell you that they're not superstitious. Well, don't believe them. What some may call superstition many Bosnians take as a natural fact. Where these beliefs have come from nobody knows in full, but rest assured the pagan Illyrians, heretic Bosnian Church, mystic rituals of eastern orthodoxy and Islam have all contributed to them. Here are just a few of the long list of superstitions....

- This one can be refuted (at least by the Bosnians) as a medical fact instead of a superstition. Drafts. Yes, drafts. All diseases are carried in drafts so if its 40 degrees outside and you see all the windows rolled up it's not because everyone has AC. Any earaches, colds, sties, headaches – well, just about any ailment is blamed on that little nip of wind from open windows. Don't be surprised to see people dashing to close the window if there is another one open in the building or car that you're in.

- Drinking anything cold is another great excuse, even in the middle of summer, for why someone is sick. Don't be disappointed, especially American travelers, to find no ice in most places. You'll get sick for heavens sake!

- Wet hair. On more than one occasion during the war one could find Sarajevans taking a brisk walk through sniper fire and shelling – that was normal. God forbid, though, if you stepped outside with wet hair. That is a big no-no. Wet hair, with the combination of wind (yes, even in the summer) will give you pneumonia, guaranteed. If the receptionist looks at you as if you've just been released from a 'home' she or he is simply worried about you. The general rule is you must first dry your hair with a hairdryer, wait at least an hour and then its safe to walk the streets. And you think I'm kidding.

- If you knock a glass over or spill something while speaking – that, of course, means its true.

- When describing an injury or sickness never ever show or explain it on your own body. Never.

- If you spill your coffee, don't fret it, it simply means you are about to be rewarded some material gain.

- An itchy left palm means you are about to get something (positive).

- An itchy right palm, naturally, means you are about to give something.

- An itchy nose means you are about to get angry.

- If you say something you would like to come true be sure to knock on wood three times, but from underneath – the underneath thing is key.

- Whenever entering a building always enter with right foot first.

- Whatever you do don't whistle in the house. It is a sure bet that you have summoned demons and when you leave there is no guarantee that they haven't.

- Bread is heaven's gift. Never throw it away. This rule gained strength in the war due to the extreme lack of food, every crumble was held in high regard.

- Always stir clockwise, it's the natural flow of things.

- It's bad luck to cut your nails after dark. Only daylight cutting please, you don't want to jinx yourself.

- Never stand in the middle of a doorframe...nobody knows why, it's just 'bad.'

- People talking about you makes you hick-up.

That's what we think you need to know to start your journey. Enjoy your trip through the next section!

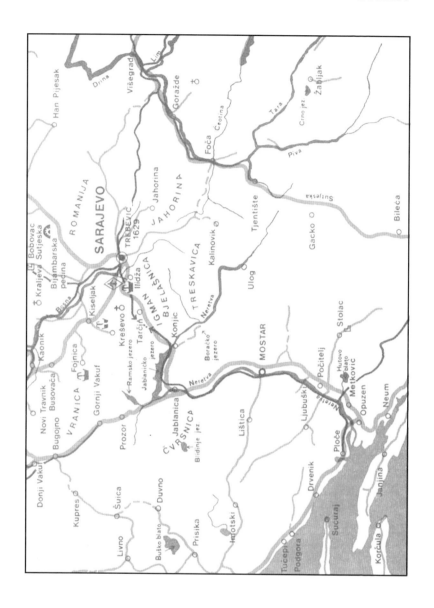

Part two: SARAJEVO

THE CITY

Sarajevo is a city in which even strangers can feel at home. Neither geographically expansive nor characterised by large buildings, the city retains a particular, arresting charm with its abundance of busy café's and abiding tradition of hospitality. The city's breathtaking backdrop of seemingly endless hills and towering mountains have in a sense always isolated the city, creating a timeless world, which despite its seclusion has always kept its doors open to the rest of the world. Although Sarajevo is a capital city typified by the hustle and bustle of everyday life, it also possesses a unique ambience that seeps into the soul.

This city epitomises a partial centuries-old struggle against outside influences combined with the absorption of these influences into one of the most diverse cultures in Europe. Whereas other parts of Bosnia and Herzegovina may still be fraught with ethnic strife, this city's long-standing tradition of multi-ethnicity enables it to thrive in its diversity. Indeed, few places on earth feature an Orthodox and a Catholic church, a mosque and a synagogue within easy walking distance of each other.

If there were any city in Europe that effortlessly straddles east and west, it is Sarajevo. Here the Byzantine and Ottoman empires of the east and the Roman, Venetian and Austro-Hungarian empires of the west left an indelible mark through culture, traditions and religions.

A walk through Sarajevo is a walk through its past. From the oriental Ottoman quarters lined with sweet shops, café's and handicraft workshops, to the administrative and cultural centre of Austro-Hungarian times, Sarajevo encompasses the very best of both worlds.

In Sarajevo, people have time for family and friends. It is often said that a man's wealth is not measured in his material belongings but rather in his friendships - here they invest the time to nurture such friendships.

What we don't know in the west

During the war I visited a family living in the mainly Muslim quarter of Bistrik. Their house was very close to the front line and we had to sit in the dark (there was no electricity anyway) so the snipers could not see us. An old man stared at me from across the room and I could see he had something to say to me. He eventually made his way across the room and said softly, 'Son, just down there in Baščaršija is a shoemaker who has a wife and two children. One morning a customer walked into his shop and asked to buy a pair of shoes. The shoemaker replied "Thank you for your business, sir, but my neighbour also makes good shoes and he too has a wife and two children. I have already sold a pair of shoes this morning, please buy from him so that he may take care of his family." The old man paused and then unaccusingly continued, "That, son, you don't know in the West. That is the way we grew up and that is how things need to be." The sense of community here is quite remarkable. It carries a piece of the past that reminds us of what it means to take care of each other and look out for our neighbours. This rule may not hold true for everyone in Baščaršija but it is these traditions that make the Sarajevo experience such a special one.

HISTORY

Surrounded by sloping mountains from both the north and south sides, Sarajevo spreads east and west as if open not only to the winds and watercourses but also to the influences of the variety of cultures flowing from these directions. Situated on the convergence of two major water basins along the valleys of the Bosnia and Neretva rivers, which connect northern Europe with the Mediterranean Sea, its location in the heart of the Balkan Peninsula served as a gateway for the peoples of Greece and Asia Minor migrating towards West Central Europe and vice versa since ancient times.

The first known human settlements date back almost 5,000 years. At Butmir (near Sarajevo International Airport) one of the most interesting and rich Neolithic findings in the Balkans was discovered. More than 90 urban settlements and a great number of tools and finely chiselled domestic utensils and pots were unearthed. As a result of this 19th-century archaeological discovery, the Neolithic culture of this area was called Butmir culture. It dates back to 2400BC.

The Illyrians lived in this territory at the end of the Bronze Age, and remains of their settlements have been located in many areas around Sarajevo. When the Romans conquered the Illyrians in the 1st century AD, they established their headquarters near the thermal springs of what is today known as Ilidža. The remains of Roman villas, baths, mosaics and sculptures can still be seen there.

When the Slavic tribes from the north arrived in the 7th century, Slav culture and state models began to dominate. In the 12th century Bosnia gradually established itself as a regional power, with its territorial expansion culminating in the 14th century. A major centre of the Bosnian state was established in the area of present-day Sarajevo, where the Vrhbosna region - with the fortified cities of Hodidjed, Kotorac and Vrhbosna as well as Trgovište - was situated.

The timeline of human settlements in the area of Sarajevo is preserved in the rich collections displayed in the National Museum of Bosnia and Herzegovina, one of the oldest scientific and cultural establishments in Sarajevo. The existence of tens of thousands of tombstones (stećak) erected

1 Ottoman era Muslim graveyard in Alifakovac

arajevo's Catholic Cathedral on rhadija Street

The famous Sebilj fountain in the heart of Sarajevo's old town

Sarajevo's new art market

The Sarajevo Film Festival ranks amongst Europe's best

Fresh spices, teas and nuts in Baščaršija

sy side-street in the old quarters

e Eternal Flame on Tito Street pays homage
the liberators of Sarajevo during WWII

Sarajevo's newest generation

Handmade local and Persian carpets in Morića Han.

by Bosnian Church followers bears evidence to medieval, heretic Bosnia and its unique artistic expressions. Some of the finest examples of this magnificent stone art can be seen in the National Museum gardens.

In the middle of the 15th century Sarajevo was annexed by the Ottoman Empire. The Ottomans asserted great influence in Sarajevo decades before Bosnia was officially conquered. In the early years after the Ottoman invasion the city of Saraj-ovasi (saraj meaning castle or palace and ovas meaning field) is mentioned for the first time. The Slavs then adapted this name to their own language and pronunciation. Sarajevo became the first Ottoman administrative and military base in Bosnia, and soon afterwards the centre of the Bosnian Sandžak (the largest territorial sub-division in the Ottoman Empire).

In this newly founded city emerged the first leather craftsmen, blacksmiths, saddlers, millers and bakers. Life in the city, both from an economical and cultural point of view, developed at an increasingly rapid pace during the 16th century. Many bridges were built over the Miljacka River that runs through the heart of the city; the Kozija ćuprija, Ćehaja and Latinska ćuprija attest to the magnificence of oriental architecture. On the right bank of the river flourished the Baščaršija quarter which became the social, economical and cultural centre of the young oriental city and the largest commercial centre in the central Balkans. The streets in Baščaršija have been named after the crafts that were practised there for centuries.

The caravans arriving from Venice, Vienna, central Europe, the Mediterranean and the east were accommodated in one of the 50 inns of Sarajevo, known as 'han'. The most famous was Morića han which was built at the end of the 16th century. Today it is a tourist attraction, offering an authentic glimpse of Sarajevo's past, but in earlier times it offered facilities such as guest rooms, a café on the first floor and a courtyard with a porch for loading and unloading goods, warehouses and horse stables.

By the 16th century the city had established regular contacts with other European cities and began to resemble a true metropolis. The first wooden-pipe waterworks were built to supply both private and public dwellings, and water fountains (šadrvani) were built in mosque courtyards and other public areas. The Turkish baths, called hamams, were constructed in authentic Ottoman style. There were seven Turkish baths in the city, the most important of which being Gazi Husrev-beg.

The vision of the city expanded with Ottoman rule and many new buildings were erected: mosques, Islamic places of worship (mesdžidi), primary and secondary school buildings (mektebi and medrese), and centres of mystic philosophy (tekija). One of the most impressive mosques in Sarajevo is Gazi Husrev-beg. It was built in 1531 and, like the town's primary Turkish bath, named after the governor of Bosnia who systematically embarked on creating a city that was often compared to Damascus.

One of the distinctive features of Ottoman rule was tolerance of other religious creeds, particularly compared to the wretched record of religious persecution by most European powers of that time. The Orthodox, Catholics and the Sephardic Jews (expelled from Spain in 1492 and resettled in Sarajevo) lived and worked together in relative harmony in the Baščaršija quarter. This laid the foundation for the cultural pluralism for which the city is known today.

The old Orthodox Church was built at the beginning of Ottoman rule and the school founded next to it was mentioned for the first time only two years after the first Muslim secondary school had been established. The church museum still hosts a great number of icons dating back to the 14th and 15th centuries. The new Orthodox cathedral erected at the end of Ottoman rule demonstrates how baroque and Russian-Orthodox trends became popular within the same cultural framework.

The old Roman Catholic Church, which had likely existed in Latinluk since the Middle Ages, was destroyed in 1697 when Prince Eugene of Savoy swept through the Bosna River Valley and burned Sarajevo to the ground. It was later rebuilt and eventually replaced by the Catholic churches erected after the Austro-Hungarian occupation of Bosnia and Herzegovina in 1878. A large number of Sarajevo's Catholic population left in fear of reprisals after the Austro-Hungarians razed the city, but the Catholic merchants' influence has never left Sarajevo.

Sarajevo is one of the few European cities that has had a water supply system for more than 400 years. In the 17th century a Turkish travel writer named Evlija Čelebi pointed out the existence of 110 drinking-water fountains in his journal.

Sarajevo experienced for the first time the full current of European culture during the 40 years of Austro-Hungarian administration. New schools and European-structured scientific institutes were opened and Sarajevo's young intellectuals were educated in major cities around Europe. The city also enjoyed strong economic, cultural and political development; the first modern industries appeared: a tobacco factory in 1880, a carpet-weaving factory in 1888, a furniture factory in 1869 and a soap factory in 1894, in addition to the power plants, textile and food industries. The first railway was also officially opened and mainly used to exploit Bosnia's rich natural resources.

Alongside these developments, there was growing resistance to yet another occupying power in Sarajevo. The rebellions in the last years of Ottoman dominion in Bosnia and Herzegovina set the stage for a strong resistance movement, much of which was focused in Sarajevo by the Bosnian Serbs and encouraged by nationalist elements in neighbouring Serbia.

On June 28 1914 a young Serbian nationalist, Gavrilo Princip, assassinated Archduke Franz Ferdinand, the Austro-Hungarian heir, and his wife Sofia. Austria then declared war on Serbia. Russia, having had its eyes on the Balkans for some time, sided with Serbia and declared war on Austria. It was this event that ignited World War I.

After World War II and victory by Tito's partisans, Sarajevo developed rapidly. The population grew considerably and the territory expanded to include ten new municipalities. Sarajevo became the artistic, cultural and spiritual heart of Bosnia and Herzegovina. The highlight of Sarajevo's emergence from its cultural and social revolution was the 1984 Winter Olympics, at that time the largest Winter Olympic Games in history.

The siege of Sarajevo: *by Jim Marshall*

The war that ravaged Sarajevo, claiming over 10,500 lives, including those of 1,600 children, began on the 5th of April, 1992. It followed weeks of instability in the city and the deployment of Yugoslavian National Army artillery to strategic points overlooking the city. On this date, two young women were shot dead by Bosnian Serb sniping during an anti-war demonstration. A small plaque on the bridge on which they were killed commemorates their death.

A number of massacres punctuated the siege, beginning with an early attack on a bread queue on the 27th of May, 1992 killing 17, through two attacks, on a football game and a water queue in June and July of 1993 leaving up to 30 dead, to the market-place massacres of 5th February, 1994 and 28th of August 1995 in which over 100 people were killed. However, the siege was principally punctuated by the routine and solitary deaths of thousands of Sarajevo's population both old and young and of all ethnicities.

Extensive destruction of the city's buildings and infrastructure were another feature and indeed objective of the military siege of Sarajevo. This was typified by the intentional targeting of non-military buildings. Those destroyed during the siege included the National Library, the Olympic Museum, the Olympic indoor arena 'Zetra', schools, religious buildings and even the city's maternity hospital.

Throughout the siege, Sarajevans lived largely without water, gas and electricity, existed on inadequate quantities of food for the duration of the war and were forced to endure a neutral international military presence (UNPROFOR) that repeatedly stood by and watched the slaughter of civilians.

For despite a U.N. presence in Sarajevo even prior to the outbreak of hostilities and a decision from the U.N. Security Council in the spring of 1993 to declare Sarajevo a "safe area", UNPROFOR troops were themselves increasingly targeted and killed by the Bosnian Serb Army as the siege dragged on.

Following the market-place shelling of 28th of August, 1995 the direct military siege of Sarajevo came to an abrupt end in the first days of September after pin point NATO bombing of Bosnian Serb army positions. All parties were called to Dayton, Ohio and the Clinton Administration brokered a peace deal that is still the framework for peace today.

Sarajevans of all ethnic backgrounds still celebrate their diversity and exercise an impressive, natural tendency to tolerance while identifying themselves as European. The churches and mosques are still frequented by their respective worshippers and the schools and university still educate a multiethnic mixture of students.

Most of Sarajevo's national and cultural monuments have now been repaired or reconstructed. Despite challenging economic and social conditions, Sarajevo is the wealthiest city in Bosnia and Herzegovina.

It is once again the centre of political, cultural and spiritual life and its tradition of hospitality has not diminished.

TOUR OPERATORS

People who want to see some of the highlights of Bosnia and Herzegovina as part of a regional tour should have no problems. Many of the operators with itineraries in Croatia offer one- or two-day trips to Bosnia and Herzegovina. If you are heading for the Croatian coast, you do not even have to make any prior arrangements for a trip to Bosnia and Herzegovina, as your hotel is probably able to arrange that trip at very short notice.

Once you are in Sarajevo, a range of operators offers guided tours through the city, hikes, and half-day and one-day trips to other cities, the country-side and nature parks. The website addresses given here are not always in English and rarely give a comprehensive overview of what the various operators offer. A visit to their offices is generally the best way to get an impression.

- **Green Visions** Radnička bb; tel/fax: 033 717 290 / 061 213 278; email: sarajevo@greenvisions.ba; web: www.greenvisions.ba. Green Visions is the leading eco-tourism group in Bosnia and Herzegovina. They promote the country's cultural and natural heritage and specialise in hiking, rafting, mountain biking, village tourism and tour skiing. Green Visions also organises field trips and research programs (geography, anthropology, ethnology, ecology, history) for schools and universities from Europe and North America. They speak English, Dutch and French.

- **Otas Travel** Maršala Tita 38; tel: 033 221 420/410; fax: 033 221 430; email: otas1958@bih.net.ba; web: www.otas.ba. Otas has been a youth travel agent for decades in the former Yugoslavia. They offer accommodation, tours and information to young travellers, and specialise in 'countryside' tours that promote domestic and organic foods. This is a good place for ISIC travellers to check out as, among other things, they have all the info on which places offer discounts for ISIC holders.

- **Avio Express** Zelenih beretki 22; tel: 033 208 333; fax: 033 208 334; email: avio-express-sjj-sales@gmk.net; web: www.avio-express.com. Avio often has great flight deals, and also organises charter flights from Europe. They offer hotel information for Sarajevo and can organise excursions outside of Sarajevo for groups and student trips.

- **City Tour** Zelenih beretki 22a; tel: 061 190 591; email: sightseeingsarajevo@europe.com. This group of young guides offers only one service and they do it well. City Tour gives three-hour city tours for individuals or groups. They are very reasonably priced and can be found at the main tourist information centre.

- **Ljubičica Tourist Agency** M. M. Bašeskije 65; tel: 033 535 829; fax: 033 232 109; email: taljubic@bih.net.ba; web: www.internet.ba/ljubica. Good for cheap accommodation, money exchange and general information. They are centrally located in Baščaršija.

- **Sar Tour** M M Bašeskije 63; tel/fax: 033 238 680; email: sartour@1sinter.net. Sar Tour can organise inexpensive accommodation for the budget traveller. They also have city guides in English and German (a two-hour city tour is 50 KM for two people).

- **Unis Tours** Ferhadija 16; tel: 033 445 037; fax: 033 209 089; email: unis-tours@internet.ba; web: www.unis-tours.ba. This is one of the oldest and best-established travel agencies in the city. Unis organises ski trips to Jahorina, Bjelašnica and Vlašić in the winter and excursions to Neum in the summer. They also have a car rental department.

- **Vertical Mountain Guide Agency** tel: 033 216 619/447 355. This agency employs a small group of very experienced hikers and climbers. If you are a serious Alpine climber, these are your men.

- **Bjelašnica Mountain Association** Zelenih beretki 15; tel: 033 535 371; email: pdbjelasnica@yahoo.com. Bjelašnica is the largest mountain association in Bosnia and Herzegovina, and offers guides and overnight stays in one of their many mountain huts on Bjelašnica and Igman mountains. Check if you can find an English speaker.

● **Kuk** Hiseta 3/2; tel/fax: 033 205 337; mobile: 061 224 899. Kuk Travel has initiated a new travel program for tour operators coming to Bosnia and Herzegovina. For group trips they have an interesting new program.

● **Rafting Tours** Kundurdžiluk bb; tel/fax: 033 233 023; mobile: 061 146 148; e-mail: raft.t@bih.net.ba. This group specializes in Tara Rafting tours in eastern Bosnia. They are based in the old town of Sarajevo and an easy and efficient way of finding a safe and responsible rafting outfit based out of Sarajevo. They are professional and have good equipment and safety gear.

Other Travel Agencies in Sarajevo

Adria Tours Ferhadija 23/2; tel/fax: 033 233 692; tel. 033 232 125; e-mail: adria@bih.net.ba; www.adria.si

Aid Tours Ferhadija 15 (Stakleni grad); fax: 033 208 652; tel. 033 658 340; e-mail: putovanja@atworks.net

Atlas Ambasador Zelenih beretki 17; tel/fax. 033 233 445; 033 233 446; e-mail: atlasbih@yahoo.de; www.atlasbih.de.vu

Bihamk Tours Maršala Tita 1; tel: 033 212 706, 033 208 440; e-mail: sales@bihamk.ba; www.bihamk.ba

Bio Tours Ferhadija 14; tel: 033 206 086, 033 206 085; fax: 033 206 087; e-mail: biotours@bih.net.ba

Biss Tours Morića han; tel: 033 236 621; fax: 033 236 620; e-mail: bbabic@bih.net.ba

Bosnia Tours Maršala Tita 54; tel/fax: 033 202 206, 033 202 207, 033 202 059; e-mail: zlatah@bosniahotels.com

Centrotrans Bus Ferhadija 16; tel/fax: 033 205 481; tel: 033 211 282; Put života 8; tel: 033 214 959, 033 214 969; Niže banje; tel: 033 532 874; tel/fax: 033 207 964; Bulevar Meše Selimovića 97; tel/fax: 033 291 310, 033 291 311; www.centrotrans.com

Nostro Azzuro Sarajevo Dr. Fetaha Bećiregovića 23a; tel: 033 523 324

Galileo Mehremića trg 1; tel/fax: 033 214 088, 033 209 935

Grasova turistička poslovnica Zelenih beretki 38; tel: 033 233 004; tel/fax: 033 447 955

Hasanbegović Company Blažuj 47; tel: 033 623 873, mobile: 061 109 181

Olimpik Tours Trgovke 43; tel: 033 232 057

Globus Dolina 2; tel: 033 268 590; fax: 033 206 298; e-mail: globusts@bih.net.ba

Gulliver Hamida Dizdara 1; tel: 033 444 111; e-mail: gulliharisa@hotmail.com

Fibula Air Travel Mula-Mustafe Bašeskije 63; tel: 033 232 523; fax: 033 272 790; e-mail: fibula@bih.net.ba; www.fibula.com

Papalina R. Abazovića 19; tel/fax: 033 521 716

Relax Tours Plato Skenderija; tel: 033 263 190; tel/fax: 033 209 012; tel/fax: 033 263 191; Zelenih beretki 22; tel/fax: 033 263 330, 033 263 331; e-mail: relaxtours@relaxtours.com; www.relaxtours.com

S Tours S.H. Muvekita 2; tel: 033 444 810; fax: 033 444 808; e-mail: slavica9@bih.net.ba

Neckar Co. Maršala Tita 50; tel: 033 261 650, 033 261 651, 033 261 661; fax: 033 261 660; e-mail: airticket@neckar.ba

Ri-ve-ri Company Hrasnička cesta 14 (Hotel Terme); tel: 033 718 460; e-mail: riveri@bih.net.ba

Promo Tours Kemala Kapetanovića bb; tel: 033 655 346; mobile: 061 184 674

Duga Dom mladih 35, tel: 033 207 044; fax: 033 727 220; e-mail: duga@infomedia.ba

Zajednica za odmor i rekreaciju Obala Kulina bana 1/I; fax: 033 667 997

Zeba Tours Put života (Aula željezničke stanice); fax: 033 455 350; Džemala Bijedića 195a; tel: 033 205 552

Zoitours Branilaca Sarajeva 23 (ski-centar); tel/fax: 033 212 028, 033 205 769

Atlantis Dalmatinska 4; tel: 033 266 430; fax: 033 266 432; www.atlantis-travel.hr; e-mail: attravel@bih.net.ba

F Design N Garaplina 10; tel: 033 441 899; fax: 033 441 899

Feković Company Put života 2; tel/fax: 033 651 325

Albatros Sagrdžije 31; tel: 033 237 050; e-mail: albatros@bih.net.ba

Vip Travels Zelenih beretki bb (Gazi Husrev-begov bezistan); tel: 033 271 800, 033 271 801, 033 443 900; e-mail: vip_t@bih.net.ba

Suno Tours Bulevar Meše Selimovića 13; tel: 033 712 561, 033 712 500; e-mail: sunotours@yahoo.com; www.sunotours.com

Mea Tours Kranjčevićeva 43; tel/fax: 033 216 511; e-mail: toursmea@bih.net.ba

GETTING AROUND

The compact city centre makes it easy and enjoyable to do most moving around on foot. Ferhadija is a famous pedestrian alley that goes through the heart of town and is always filled, day or night, with pedestrians of all ages. Next to the river, the Vilsonovo šetalište or 'Wilson's Walkway' is closed to vehicles after 17.00. It is a popular spot for lovers taking up a park bench, rollerbladers cruising up and down, and animal lovers walking their pets. For one of the best nature walks immediately next to down-town Sarajevo, go to the swimming pool and follow the road. Only one warning for pedestrians: be aware that zebra crossings and green traffic lights do not necessarily mean it is safe to cross the street.

The local bus system is the best in the country. It runs until midnight and will get you to even the most isolated villages on Bjelašnica. The 31e buses are the handiest of all. They run through the entire length of the city every half hour and cost 1.20 KM (0.30 KM cheaper than all other buses) irrespective of the length of travel. Starting by the National Archives and finishing in Dobrinja by the airport, this is the quickest, cleanest and easiest bus route in town.

The trams constantly run up and down the main east-west road. There is also a tram station at the main bus/train station that operates all day and most of the night. The tram lines extend all the way to Ilidža, a suburb to the west of Sarajevo, and for budget travellers it is a great way to check out the Bosna River Springs and the park in Ilidža - it costs only 1.50KM one way or you can buy a day pass for 4KM (valid on all trams, buses and minibuses – except for the 31e buses). Beware of pickpockets.

Taxis are quickest. They are easy to find and cheap, with a starting fare of 1KM and another 1KM for each additional kilometre. With a few exceptions a taxi ride to anywhere in Sarajevo shouldn't cost more than 12-15KM – and for most trips you will spend less than 5KM. Waiting for an empty taxi will rarely take you more than a minute. Alternatively, 24-hour taxi stands are located all over town, or you can phone 1515.

With taxis, buses and trams everywhere, there is really no need to go into town by car. Driving can be hectic – especially from 08.00 to 10.00 and from 15.00 to 17.00 – and parking in the centre of town is often problematic. As so many others set the example, you may be tempted to park in a spot where it's explicitly forbidden. That is a risky thing to do, as the 'pauk' (spider) is on regular patrol and will tow your car away without letting you know. It will cost 120KM to get your vehicle back. It is wiser to pay 1 or 2KM per hour for a guarded parking spot. That also avoids the risk of a stolen car. You will find them simply by looking for the **P** symbol. I you don't want to waste time searching for that **P**, and you don't mind walking for a bit, you could park your car next to Skenderija or next to the Holiday Inn.

Rent-a-car

It is obviously nice to get around and see the country on your own time and at your own pace. But beware: compared to other modes of transport, a rented car is relatively costly. These are the major rental agencies. I would check a number of them out before making a choice. Fender benders and stupid driving is rather par for the course here and if you have the option of paying a little more for insurance – I suggest you take it.

Adisson Co Terezije bb, 033 203 306
AVIS rent a car Hamdije Čemerlića 2, 033 230 180
Budget Kranjčevićeva 33, 033 268 190
Champion Auto Rent Hamdije Kreševljakovića bb, 033 211 207
Europcar Branilaca Sarajeva 21, 033 217 325
Galileo Mehmeda Spahe 1, 033 209 935
Hertz Zmaja od Bosne 6, 033 204 090
MAX Auto Kranjčevićeva bb, 033 267 590
Neckar Maršala Tita 50, 033 261 650
Peugeot Feroelektro Kranjčevićeva 25, 033 216 298

Bus information

Timetable for Federation buses departing from the bus/railway station

Bihać (daily at 07.30, 13.30 and 22.00), Bugojno (daily at 10.00, 14.00, 17.30 and 19.00), Goražde (daily at 08.00), Gradačac (daily at 08.30 and

17.00), Mostar (daily at 07.00, 07.15, 09.00, 10.00, 14.30, 18.00 and 21.00), Orašje via Tuzla (daily at 06.30), Orašje via Zenica (daily at 15.30), Tešanj (daily at 07.00, 13.15 and 17.15), Tuzla (Mon-Fri at 05.00, 06.30, 08.30, 09.30 and daily at 10.30, 11.30, 12.30, 13.30, 14.00, 15.00, 15.35, 16.00, 16.30, 17.00 and 18.00), Zenica (daily at 06.30, 07.30, 08.30, 09.30, 10.30, 11.30, 12.30, 13.30, 14.30, 15.15, 16.30, 17.30, 18.30 and 19.30).

Timetable for cross-entity buses departing from the bus/railway station
Banja Luka (daily at 09.15 and 15.30), Bijeljina (daily at 05.00 and 15.00), Bosanski Brod (daily at 12.15), Bosanka Dubica (daily at 14.30), Hrenovica (daily at 07.00 and 16.30), Pale (daily at 07.00, 08.00, 10.00, 14.00, 15.00 and 16.30), Zvornik (daily at 15.30) and to Brčko (daily at 06.30 and 15.35).

   In the Dobrinja quarter of southeast Sarajevo near the airport is the East Sarajevo bus station that has regular buslines to most major destinations in the Republika Srpska. They have several daily buses to Belgrade as well. From town it is a 10 KM taxi ride or one can take the 31e bus from town to the last stop in Dobrinja - the station is only a 3 minute walk from there.

TOURIST INFORMATION

Good information is a bit hard to come by anywhere in the country. There is only one main tourist information centre in Sarajevo, located in the centre not far from the Catholic cathedral (tel: 033 220 721; fax: 033 532 281; email: tour.off@bih.net.ba; web: www.sarajevo-tourism.com). If you're standing with your back to the cathedral continue straight down the walkway past Central Café and turn left on Zelene beretke. The address is 22a and it is 50m down on the right-hand side. Information about hotels, museums, excursions, city tours and other activities is all readily available. The staff speak English, German, Turkish and French and will go out of their way to help. An up-to-date website on events in the city can be found at www.city.ba. The International Women's Club of Sarajevo has produced a well-made practical 'mini' guide to Sarajevo called "Opening Doors to Sarajevo, a Selected Guide." It's worth the 10 KM this booklet costs. Profits are donated to a good cause.

WHERE TO STAY

There are now over 40 hotels in and around the city centre. Most are in the first and tourist class, but in recent times the local people in Sarajevo have begun to pay more attention to the needs of backpackers as well. Ljubučica Travel Agency in the heart of the old town (just near pigeon square) now has Sarajevo's first youth hostel. It's not official – but there are a few hundred beds available either at the hostel or in private accommodation close to the old town. The prices are very affordable (16-24KM per night – without breakfast) and from all the feedback I've received the rooms are clean and people feel safe. There are others offering private accommodation as well. Don't pay more than 30KM per night. I've had some friends get duped for 60KM a night for a bed in someone's home. Feel free to negotiate and walk away if you're not happy.

   If you're like me, a thirty something who likes the quiet of the mountains and has a limited budget – I suggest Dom Faletići. It's a short busride to the northeast of town, only five kilometres from the pigeon square. They have a beautiful deck alongside a freshwater stream. It's quiet, the rooms are nice and affordable and there is a 1.20 KM busride to town every hour. You can take nice walks uphill in the morning or just take the road behind the motel up the one-lane asphalt road – you'll find villagers and weekenders alike tending the gardens, drinking coffee in the yard, or caring for their animals. It's quite a nice way to start the morning when on holiday – slow, good coffee, peace and quiet, warm shower. Check it out under tourist accommodation.

Business class

Hotel Grand Muhameda ef. Pandže 7; tel: 033 205 444, fax: 033 205 866. Located just behind the train station in the Velešići area, this is one of the nicest hotels in town and is known for its quality and attentive service. The rooms are fully equipped and rates for single/double rooms are reasonably priced at 120/190KM per night. The location isn't ideal if you want to be in the heart of the city and be able to walk everywhere.

Hotel Bosnia Kulovića 9, tel: 033 471 251, fax: 033 656 767; email: bosniahotel@bosniahotels.com. For those of you who might have visited Sarajevo before the war: this is the former Hotel Beograd. Although the name has changed, not much else has. The hotel is centrally located which makes getting around by foot very easy. The rooms are nice with the standard accessories. The hotel has a restaurant and café. The restaurant serves good food, particularly the traditional Bosnian meals. Rates for foreigners are higher than for locals. The cost of a single room lies around 175KM. It's 225KM per night for a double. Apartments cost around 250/300KM a night for two people.

Hotel Europa Garni Vladislava Skarića 3, tel: 033 232 855/851, fax: 033 232 860; email: europa-garni@smartnet.ba. Centrally located and recently renovated, Europa Garni is a tiny but chic hotel. The rooms are cosy with tasteful decor and its location provides peace and quiet from traffic. It is just behind the Ferhadija walkway, which is busy but never too loud. All rooms have satellite TV, minibar and AC. Single: 180KM, double: 280KM, suite: 400KM.

Hotel Dardanija Radićeva 19; tel: 033 213 613/614; fax: 033 213 616; email: dardanija@hotmail.com. Dardanija is just behind the Sarajka Mall on Maršal Tito Street. There is a general lack of parking space if you've come by car but the location is convenient for walking to most places. This small 12-room hotel is quiet and comfortable. There is a restaurant and café in the hotel. Single: 120KM, double: 200KM.

Hotel Saray Nevjestina 5; tel: 033 237 810; fax: 033 472 691; email: hotsaray@bih.net.ba; web: www.hotelsaray.com. Hotel Saray certainly has bragging rights when it comes to the best view in town. Located just outside of Baščaršija on the hill behind Bentbaša, this popular hotel just keeps getting more popular. A new wing has been added recently, increasing its capacity almost twofold. It offers all the services you can get in Sarajevo: rooms with minibar, phone, AC and satellite TV; restaurant and café; airport pick-up and drop-off; internet connections etc. A single room goes for 80KM and a double for 160KM.

Hotel Villa Orient Oprkanj 6; tel: 033 232 702; fax: 033 441 044. If you are looking to get away from the traditional hotel look and feel, then this 'villa' is it. Orient is located in the heart of the old town. Its structure is more like a downtown house than a hotel yet it offers all of the comforts you'd find in other places. The rooms are newly decorated and the whole building has a classy feel to it. Single: 150KM, double: 200KM, suite: 250KM.

Hotel Astra Zelenih beretki 9; tel: 033 252 100/200; fax: 033 209 939; email: h.astra@bih.net.ba; web: www.hotel-astra.com.ba. Astra is one of the new places in town. The place is well done inside and the decor is quite classy. They managed, however, to build a hotel in a somewhat small area and it can seem a bit cramped. The rooms are great as is the service and its location is one of the most convenient around. If you don't mind smaller spaces it's well worth a look. Single: 180KM, double: 280KM, apartment: 400KM.

Holiday Inn Zmaja od Bosne 4; tel/fax: 033 288 000. The hotel was built for the Olympics in the early 1980s. The national restaurant has good food and the café at the back of the hotel is quite fancy and a good place to do business. The rooms are the standard Holiday Inn rooms. The service is decent but often in the socialist manner, when and how they like. It is a major hub for businessmen who come to town. Single rooms are 200KM and doubles go for 300KM. They also have fancy apartments that run from 400KM to 1,300KM per night. If you're a tourist and are looking to spend wisely, there are plenty of other less expensive hotels with the same comforts.

Hotel Meridijan Jaroslava Černija 3; tel: 033 446 177 – centrally located near the Cathedral it's a small but nice place. Single: 150KM, double: 200KM, apartment: 200/250KM.

Hotel Belvedere Višnjik 2; tel: 033 262 140. It's a bit up the hill by the Koševo hospital but is an easy walk to town. The rooms are nice and clean. Single: 120/150KM, double: 150/200KM.

Hotel Italia Pofalička 7; tel: 033 650 450. For those of you who don't mind being a bit out of town this hotel is a favourite. The rates are very reasonable and the hotel has nice and new facilities. It's located just around the corner from the Sarajevo Tobacco Factory in Pofalići. Single: 90/130KM, double: 150KM, apartment: 190/240/290KM for one, two and three persons respectively.

Hotel Palas Krivajska 1; tel: 033 655 782. Hotel Palas is near the Italia and also is a favourite amongs the good deal hotels out of the center of the city. The rates are good and the hotel has conference and meeting room facilities where many groups hold seminars and conferences. The rooms are simple but nice. The hotel is within walking distance to the bus and train station. Single: 70/80KM, double: 100/110KM, apartment: 130/180KM.

Hotel Aqua Blažuj bb; tel: 033 625 500. This hotel is a good bit out of town but has brand new facilities, a work-out room, and a very nice indoor pool. The rooms are air conditioned and the service is quite good. Be warned though, there are frequent concerts that attract large crowds and a lot of noise. If you are looking for place to swim and relax during your stay, ask the reception if there are any concerts going on during your stay. Single: 85KM, double: 130KM, apartment: 180KM.

Hotel Una Stupska 2; tel: 033 775 270. This hotel too is a bit out of town and not in the nicest location. However, it has great service, an outdoor pool and an indoor tennis court. The rooms are modern with a mini-bar and sat television. Single: 100KM, double: 160KM, apartment: 250KM.

Tourist class

Bašcaršija Pansion Veliki ćurčiluk 41; tel: 033 232 185; mobile: 061 177 952. This is the closest thing to a bed and breakfast in the heart of Bašcaršija. The rooms are very nice and clean and the front desk is super helpful and friendly. You can often sit with the owner at night over a drink as he plays guitar and sings Bosnian songs. They thoroughly enjoy their work and it makes your stay that much more special. Prices include breakfast and the staff are more than willing to share information with you. It's a father-and-son-run hostel, very much in the Bašcaršija tradition of passing trades on from one generation to the next. Be prepared to take your shoes off before entering the stairwell to your room - the no-shoes policy of most Muslim homes applies here as well. They will have slippers waiting for you. Single: 60KM, double: 100KM, apartment: 120KM.

Hotel Maršal Bjelašnica; tel: 033 279 100/200; fax: 033 279 149; email: marshal@pksa.com.ba. Although it's a bit far if you want to be in Sarajevo a lot, Maršal is an inexpensive place with lovely brand-new rooms, about 25km from the centre of town. It is located at the base of the ski lifts on Bjelašnica Mountain, and built in a style that strikingly contrasts its surroundings. The hotel is a bit dead in the summer months but it comes to life in winter and reservations are hard to get. They have been working on a plan with the local tourism association to promote the Bjelašnica highland villages more throughout the spring and summer months. The peace and quiet of the mountains is a pleasant change from the compact quarters of downtown (don't forget that I'm a mountain guy though and most people absolutely love the busy quarters in downtown Sarajevo). The rooms are very reasonably priced at 55KM for a single and 80KM for a double room. In the ski season, prices go up quite a lot and vary per week.

Hotel Emona Bentbaša 11; tel: 033 272 660/271 661; fax: 033 271 662. This is a cosy place just outside the old town in Bentbaša. It is a 3-minute walk to the heart of the old town. This family-owned hotel is small but has nice rooms and very friendly service. The rooms have AC, phone and satellite TV. There is also an internet connection in the hotel. Breakfast is included in the price of 100-133KM for a single and 156KM for a double.

Guest House Halvat Kasima ef. Dobrače 5; tel/fax: 033 237 714/715; email: halvat@bih.net.ba; web: www.halvat.com.ba. This is a popular spot with young and thirty-something travellers, although not exclusively for them. The Halvat House is near the old town and offers small but comfortable accommodation. Prices for a single are 89KM and doubles go for 119KM. There is quite a friendly atmosphere about the place and previous guests always seem to come back.

Dom Faletići Faletići 4; tel: 033 240 710; fax: 033 240 711. Dom Faletići is the only hotel in town set in the hills above Sarajevo. The mountain setting is still only a 10-minute drive to the centre of the old town. The hotel is new with basic rooms, a restaurant and café. The building is in traditional style with wooden balconies and stone foyers. It's a bargain for 48KM per single and only 80KM for a double. They also have an apartment for 100KM per night. They provide airport pick-up. If you are in town and trying to find your way there, the owner of Hotel Astra is the brother of Dom Faletići and they'll gladly point you in the right direction.

Konak Pansion Mula-Mustafe Bašeskije 48; tel: 033 533 506. This place is being renovated and the hotel license and telephone number has temporarily gone to a house directly across the street. There is no sign at all. Just knock on the door or phone the owner if you can't find it. The rooms are extremely basic, hostel style, and cost 40KM for a single and 60KM for a double.

PI Students' Centre Radićeva 6; tel: 033 205 231/663 355; email: student_hotel@yahoo.com. This is the closest thing in the city to a youth hostel. The student dormitories that are not used during the summer are open for students (and non-students). It's best to email ahead of time to confirm that they are open. The Students' Centre seems to prefer catering for groups.

Motel Mejdan Mustaj-pašin mejdan 11; tel: 033 233 563; single: 80KM, double: 120KM.

Pansion Zem Zem Mula-Mustafe Bašeskije 61; tel: 033 239 648; single: 40KM, double: 80KM.

Motel Amerika Himzarina 23; tel: 033 679 345; single: 100KM, double: 160KM.

Pansion Čobanija Čobanija 29; tel: 033 441 749; single: 80KM, double: 120KM.

Motel Maksi Azize Šaćirbegović 40; tel: 033 713 651; single: 85KM, double: 130KM.

Prenoćište Sinovi Drine Put života bb; tel: 033 445 651; single: 25KM, double: 52KM.

Pansion Melli Safeta Zajke 229; tel: 033 468 776; single: 33KM, double: 56KM.

Hotel Imzit Lukavička cesta 121; tel: 033 451 423; single: 70KM, double: 120KM.

Motel Orijent Bačići bb; tel: 033 468 327; single: 40KM, double: 80KM.

Prenoćište Banana City Džemala Bijedića bb; tel: 033 464 200; single: 30KM, double: 60KM.

*In the suburb of **Ilidža**, there are some excellent hotels in very nice locations. From Ilidža it is not far from Sarajevo center. Look a bit further in the Ilidža section of this guide.

WHERE TO EAT AND DRINK

Sarajevo is not a land of gourmet international cuisine. However, the food in Sarajevo is very good and generally quite inexpensive – even in the so-called expensive places. Most restaurants will serve traditional foods – which range from thick stews to veal medallion's to Viennese snitzel (don't forget the Austrians ruled here for some time, as did the Ottomans, and both left their cuisine trail behind them). There are too many good places to name in this guide but we've highlighted some of the best for you. For the vegetarians amongst us – we've prepared a little special somethin' for you.

First class restaurants

Vinoteka Skenderija 12; tel: 033 214 996. Near the Skenderija Mall, this brand-new restaurant has large windows and a classically chic decor.

The excellent menu is largely Italian and the cook uses fresh ingredients. The service is first class. In the basement is a wine bar with the finest selection of international wines in town. Main courses range from 12KM to 25KM.

Park prinčeva Iza Hrida 7; tel: 033 222 708; website: www. parkprinceva.ba. Dazzles with not only the best view in town but great food and live traditional music. The service is first class with a good wine selection and great traditional meals.

Sarajevska pivara Franjevačka 15; tel: 033 239 740. Sarajevo's famous brewery is located in the old town quarter of Bistrik near St. Ante's church. This brewery has a recent and rather pleasant addition – a new restaurant and brewery pub that serves excellent food and a new type of local brew: the only dark beer made in Bosnia and Herzegovina. The service is fantastic and the interior is amongst the nicest in the whole country. It's a must visit during your stay in Sarajevo, even if it's just for a pint.

Dubrovnik Logavina 9; tel: 033 447 830/831; fax: 033 447 829. This represents the age-old ties between these two cities. Offers fine Mediterranean cuisine and wines. It has an intimate atmosphere to match its great service. It's a local favourite of the diplomatic corps residing in the capital city. Reservations recommended.

Gaj Skenderija 14; tel/fax: 033 445 200; email: info@hotel-gaj.co.ba; web: www.hotel-gaj.co.ba. This holds a tradition from the early '70s as a place where friends gather to talk and eat. It has changed its exterior look but still maintains its friendly face. They serve mainly traditional and Italian cuisine and also have a good selection of salads and wines.

Jezz Zelenih beretki 14; tel: 033 650 312. Situated in a basement without windows, this restaurant is an expat's favourite. The menu is international, the food is excellent and the serice is friendly.

La Familija Maršala Tita 12; tel: 033 666 774/213 335. This transforms from a relatively expensive lunch spot to a fine dining experience in the evening. The salad bar and soups can't be beaten and the evening menu offers tasty Italian, French and local dishes. It's a favourite place for the diplomatic corps. Save room for desert - the home-made apple crumble with vanilla sauce is simply delicious.

Plavi zamak Zvornička 25; tel: 033 657 192. Another favourite of the diplomatic corps. It's hard to go wrong with this traditional dining experience. The service is excellent and the food and wine is even better. Remarkably for such an upmarket place, this restaurant is very child-friendly, and on quiet days the waiters will play with your children.

To Be ~~Or Not~~ To Be Ćizmedžiluk 5; tel: 033 233 265. This is one of Sarajevo's best-kept secrets. This tiny eatery, on a quiet side street, has a superb ambience for a romantic dinner in downtown Sarajevo. The menu is created from the owners' collection of recipes from around Europe. They offer several hearty vegetarian meals and the fantastic soups are made from scratch.

Marijin Dvor Zmaja od Bosne (near the Holiday Inn). With over 100 years of tradition this landmark meeting place has been a local favourite since the Austro-Hungarian times. The great food is enhanced by the art nouveau ambience. The host recommends the steak and seafood dishes.

Dom pisaca Kranjčevića 24; tel: 033 471 158. This is a rather well-known writers club that offers fine dining in Marijin Dvor just behind the twin towers buildings. The menu is standard and the food is very good. They have a decent wine list and the atmosphere is quite relaxing.

Tourist class restaurants

Mash Eat Club Branilaca Sarajeva 21 (centre); tel: 063 489 033. The hottest eatery in town is a hip place for the uptown socialites and downtown socialisers. They offer a unique menu of dishes from Mexico to the Mediterranean, and will even pamper you with weekend champagne brunches. Do check it out.

Metropolis Maršala Tita 21 (centre); tel: 033 203 315; 033 203 265. One of Sarajevo's best providers of cosmopolitan food, offering breakfast and great salads. Choose your own sauce dishes and mouthwatering cakes and ice-cream. You should visit this place at least once during your stay.

Inat kuća Veliki Alifakovac 1 (old town); tel: 033 447 867. Perhaps the finest offer of Bosnian cuisine in town. Do try the begova čorba (beg's soup), it is said to be the best in town. It's truly a great taste of local food in an authentically Bosnian ambience. The service tends to be rather slow so if you're in a hurry, skip it.

Lovački dom Nahorevsko bb, Nahorevo (surrounding hills). Set in the Nahorevo Valley this traditional restaurant has set the standard for home-made cooking. It is only a short 15-minute drive north from the city centre, in a gorgeous valley surrounded by mountains. Grilled lamb, trout, beignets and young cheese are house favourites.

Kod Bibana Hošin brijeg (Hrid); tel: 033 232 026. If you're looking for a beautiful view and simple and inexpensive traditional food, take the taxi ride up to Bibana on Hrid.

Željo Bravadžiluk bb (old town); tel: 033 447 000 or 033 441 200. Most locals will say you haven't visited Sarajevo until you've tried Željo's famous ćevapi (lamb and beef sausages). They are so popular that they've opened up two shops right next to each other. Depending on portion size ćevapi with a drink runs from 6KM to 8KM.

Sahara Hamdije Kreševljakovića, has a strange theme to it...serving pasta dishes and Thai food. Both are good eatin'. They also serve other Asian dishes. It is, as far as I know, the only place with Thai food made with coconut milk. If you're missing a taste of the fareast, western style – go here.

Ćevabdžinica Bosna Bravadžiluk bb (old town). The traditional pita dish can be found all over Bosnia and Herzegovina and particularly in Sarajevo's old town. Migrant Albanians from Macedonia and Kosovo are famous for their bakeries and pita places - Bosna is amongst the best around. A portion of pita with home-made yoghurt starts at 3KM. It's good eating ... and it's cheap.

Imidž Semizovac bb (Semizovac town); tel: 033 436 437. A bit out of the way but certainly worth the drive. Located near the town of Semizovac in an all-natural setting, this is certainly one of the finest traditional restaurants around. It's a 30-minute drive from the centre of town on the main road towards Olovo. There is a playground for children (and an open-air swimming pool twenty minutes further down that street).

Borselino Terezije bb (centre, on the Skenderija shopping centre plateau); tel: 033 216 949. By far the best crepe place in town. Reasonably priced with great service, this father and son business has mastered the art of crepe making. There is an outdoor summer terrace and in winter the restaurant is well heated and ventilated. Crepes run from 3KM and a main-course meal will cost around 10KM.

Avlija Čekaluša 64a (Mejtaš); tel: 033 444 483. Meaning garden, this is a great little place for inexpensive food and drink. They serve mainly sandwiches and burgers with a few salads to choose from. The atmosphere is always a comfy, laid-back one and both locals and ex-pats frequent it.

Karuzo Ulica Dženetića čikma (near the Catholic cathedral and just behind the open fruit and veg market); tel: 033 444 647. Perhaps the only non-smoking restaurant in town. The chef, Sasha, is excellent and very friendly. They cater well to vegetarians and seafood lovers (including sushi). It's a small but comfy place - good food, good price. Do not go there if you are in a hurry.

Curry Grbavička 4; tel: 033 217 374. Although the name may suggest a tasty curry meal, don't let that fool you. Curry does, however, have a great menu (very vegetarian friendly) with good pasta dishes and soups and a better than average selection of salads.

Galata Saray Baščaršija (old town) is just off the Ferhadija walkway and, believe it or not, is the only NON SMOKING restaurant in the city. They serve traditional food in the traditional way and you won't get choked by the annoying cigarette smoke that often billows from many other restaurants in town.

Bock Musala bb; tel: 063 454 852. Although this may be a bit hard to find, those who search will be glad they did. This new restaurant changes its menu daily, serves good French wines, and has a price list that will make any budget traveler come back again and again. It shares an entrance with Bock club on the side street behind the presidency. The chef Dario speaks English and Italian….and of course the international language of excellent food where no words are necessary.

OTHER RESTAURANTS WORTH CHECKING OUT

Bazeni Bentbaša bb; tel: 033 441 240
Broadway Kranjčevićeva 11; tel: 033 211 023
Cedar Hadžiristićeva bb; tel: 033 209 789
Ham Ali-pašina 201; tel: 033 678 824
La Guitara Gabelina 25; tel: 033 217 408
Lira Pehlivanuša 1; tel: 033 668 466
Lovac Petrakijina 24; tel: 033 664 176
Magnum Kranjčevića 18; tel: 033 213 334
Manager club Kranjčevića 13; tel: 033 613 748
Zelena dolina Partiotske lige 56; tel: 033 208 050
Cappuccino Grbavička; tel: 033 523 637

PIZZERIAS

Bambus Ferhadija bb; tel: 033 442 541
Casper Ciglanska 2; tel: 033 205 100
Diablo Dr. Mustafe Pintola 2; tel: 033 621 998

Dino Braće Mulić bb; tel: 033 234 266
Galija Čobanija 20; tel: 033 443 350
MT Velika avlija 3; tel: 033 538 086
Oskar Patke 1; tel: 033 533 222
Papagaj Hamdije Kreševljakovića 61; tel: 033 213 133
Pizza Hot Ferhadija 5; tel: 033 211 202

Veggies and Vegans

Although Sarajevo is not a veggie stronghold, there are some basic traditional dishes or snacks which are meat free and available in most restaurants and fast food outlets.

Traditional veggie options
Sirnica – cheese pie
Zeljanica – spinach pie
Pohovani sir – breaded cheese
Maslenica – dough and cheese (very oily)
Krompiruša – potato pie
Tikvenica – pumpkin pie
Grah bez mesa – beans without meat

The 'pie' is in fact a doughy-folded-filo-pastry-like bed in which the additional ingredients are tucked.

Salads that are normally vegetarian are
Valdof salata – waldorf salad
Francuska salata – French salad
Šopska salata – tomato, cucumber, onion salad and Travnik cheese
Sezonska salata – season salad – e.g. winter – sauerkraut, pickles etc

Polenta (or palenta or pura)
Polenta is traditionally served with yoghurt and is often made with milk and costs only a few KMs

Corn-ish delight
There are many corn-on-the-cob vendors throughout the city, charging 1KM a piece. The corn is usually a little sweet and eaten au naturel or with salt. A good corn guy cooks his cobs by the fountain outside the Gazi Husrev-beg mosque in the old town. He comes recommended by locals and the golden nugget I had from him was huge, perfectly cooked and delicious.

Crepes/pancakes

You can buy various types of pancake around the city. **Borselino** on Terezije bb is the best of the bunch.

Self Catering

Alternatively, if you have access to a kitchen (some room renters may let you use their kitchen and it's always worth asking if you need to pinch pennies), there is a good supermarket on each side of the river.

On the north side there is the 24 hour **MaxMarket drugstore**, which unfortunately does not offer cross dressing options but does stock a reasonable range of veggie foodstuffs. It is situated on Mula-Mustafe Bašeskije 3, just on the left fork of the road after the Eternal Flame at the end of Marsala Tita. There are beans, lentils, vegetable pates including a kidney bean variety (which was new to me), soya products like the rehydratable chunks you seem to be able to get all over the Balkans, and polenta. You can also get a range of breads which may suit a gluten free diet (pumpernickel, sunflower seed and other dark breads, for example).

On the south side there is mini-market **Heljić** at Zelenih beretki 28. It has many soya based products, burgers, sausages and chunks, tofu feta cheese, polenta in many guises, vegetable pates, vegetable juices, seeds and beans. There is a small diabetic food range, bio (organic) products, diet foods, speciality breads (rye, German rottenbrot) and non-dairy drink products like rice or oatmeal milk. They have soya, salsa and tamari sauces and many spices to liven-up your home-cooking. There is also a fine selection of pet food (!).

Markets

There is an outdoor fruit and veg market accessed from Mula-Mustafe Bašeskije, behind the Catholic cathedral. Dairy and fish products can be found in the golden orange coloured indoor market across the street. The market is open all year daytime only.

Helpful Phrases

I can't/don't eat dairy produce – Ne mogu jesti mliječne proizvode/ Ne jedem mliječne proizvode i jaja

I am allergic to nuts – Alergičan sam na orahe

I am diabetic – Ja sam dijabetičar

I can't eat wheat products – Ne mogu jesti pšenične proizvode / Ne jedem

I have a gluten allergy – Imam alergiju na gluten

I don't eat meat – Ne mogu jesti meso /Ne jedem meso

I don't eat fish – Ne mogu jesti ribu /Ne jedem ribu

Is there any meat in this? – Ima li mesa u ovome

> **Is there any dairy produce in this**? – Ima li mliječnih proizvoda
> ili jaja u ovome
>
> (puter – butter, jaja – eggs, mlijeko – milk, meso – meat, riba -
> fish)

Café's and bars

Karabit (centre). One of the newest places in town, next to the National Gallery across from Trg Oslobođenja, and a popular hangout for artists and the creative crowd. The best selections in town of fresh juices, organic Moroccan teas, and coffees. I t's a hip spot, but not at all full of itself. Check out the bookstore section and have a read over a coffee.

Jezz Zelenih beretki 14 (centre). A fantastic location in an old Austro-Hungarian-era cellar. There is often live jazz music and always a great atmosphere - very much a thirty-something crowd.

City Pub (old town). Perhaps the most-happening new place in town. It recently converted from a Lebanese restaurant to a city bar. They did, however, keep the restaurant's menu and it is still the only place in town to serve falafel, hummus and all those yummy dishes from the Middle East. It's a great lunch spot during the day and at night is quite packed with a good mix of foreign and local hipsters.

buybook Radićeva 4 (centre). This café, book and music store is where many of the local writers and artists hang out. It is a very laid-back place and you're more than welcome to grab a book and read while drinking your coffee. The music selection is always a step ahead of the rest.

Meeting Point Hamdije Kreševljakovića 13 (centre). The main location during the Sarajevo Film Festival, it's a great local hangout, usually for the 20-30 year olds.

so.ba Obala Maka Dizdara bb (centre). Located in the Arts Academy, so you know what to expect. There is always hopping electronic music and there are several computers with internet connections upstairs for 1KM an hour.

The Bar (centre). A bit pricier but one of the best summer bars in town. Lounge out on the cool couches under the large oak trees. In the winter the downstairs club is great with frequent live music gigs.

Ćulhan (old town). The 'for-everyone' café in Baščaršija. Situated in the heart of the old town it's a great outdoor café for the spring and summer months. It's closed when the cold weather comes.

Guinness Pub (old town). No town would be complete without an Irish pub and the Guinness Pub is the best one in town. Located just off the Ferhadija walkway it serves many foreign beers and has Guinness, naturally, on tap.

Boemi Valtera Perića 16 (centre). The late nightclub for dancing; they have theme nights as well including flamenco dancing. It's a popular place, which means it's crowded and smoky.

Clou (centre). A jazz club for the diehard jazzers who love small, cellar-like bars with great local sounds. Expect two things: a great time and to smell of smoke.

Terra Sacra Another small local dive that often has live jazz or blues. It's a tiny cellar-bar that always has good music and is more or less a pure local hangout.

Sloga Mehmeda Spahe 20 (centre). The 'mecca' of old-school Sarajevo bars and clubs. With three floors you'll find a more folk and acoustic touch on the first floor; on floor number two is the concert hall and bar where local and foreign bands play every week; the third floor is dedicated to the Yugo-nostalgics. Cheap beer and old-school, simple service is what you'll get - an authentic taste of a pre-war bar in Sarajevo.

Oscar Merhemića trg 14 (centre). The place to go if you like cocktails. The owner and bartender was both the Yugoslav and the Bosnian champion cocktail mixer.

Morića han Sarači 77 (old town). Where traders and travellers stayed in Ottoman times during their visit to Sarajevo. Now it offers a traditional taste of the old world. There are several café's and a restaurant inside. They also sell authentic Persian and local rugs here. Don't be afraid to bargain with them.

HARP Pub The only genuine Irish bar in town. The owner is from the south of Ireland and most of his customers are the British Embassy folks. They have a satellite dish with all the football matches and serve a proper breakfast. It's a 10KM taxi ride from the centre.

Zlatna ribica just around the corner from Bennetton is one of the newest bars in town and it has proved to be quite popular. It's got a smooth and groovy blues feel to it.

Buddha bar next to the Robna kuća on Radićeva Street is a nice chill place with relaxing Asian décor. The music is excellent and not too loud. Ease down the corridor before slipping into Sarajevo's only Asian theme bar.

OTHER CAFÉ'S AND BARS WORTH CHECKING OUT...

Atrium Ferhadija 14a; tel: 033 651 758

Babaloo Kranjčevićeva 19; tel: 033 208 595

Brasil Dalmatinska 2; tel: 033 666 000

Caballo Himze Polovine 37; tel: 033 221 819

Central Café Štrosmajerova bb; tel: 033 200 442

Galerija Ferhadija 1; tel: 033 210 205

Gradska kafana Fra Grge Martića 4; tel: 033 207 961

Kačako Koševo 34; tel: 033 444 490

Marquee Obala Kulina bana – dark place with lots of rock and roll!

Kangaroo Štrosmajerova bb; tel: 033 220 356

Kod Goge Ali-pašina; tel: 033 663 349

Kogo Dalmatinska 2; tel: 033 213 465

Le Figaro Zmaja od Bosne; tel: 033 659 732

Leonardo café Azize Šaćirbegović; tel: 033 257 957

Manhattan Kulovića 15; tel: 033 204 498

Michelle Ferhadija 25; tel: 033 444 484

No1 Husrefa Radžića 20

Park Maršala Tita 11; tel: 033 210 657

Clubs

AG club Patriotske lige 20; tel: 033 278 493
Barhana Džulagina čikma 8; tel: 061 365 408
Rock Teatar Valtera Perića 10
Urban Loco club Tekija čikma bb
X café Kranjčevićeva 1; tel: 033 220 605

Casinos

Admiral Kulovića 7; tel: 033 650 459
Coloseum club Terezije b.b.; tel: 033 250 860. Not only is this place the nicest casino in town with excellent service but there is a small theatre inside where they hold great concerts – you can sit, drink and dine to some of Sarajevo's best music.

Sweet shops

Palma Ribara 5 (Grbavica); tel: 033 234 775, 033 659 261. Old traditions never die in Sarajevo. Palma is its most prestigious café/sweet shop. Amidst the shrapnel-ridden buildings of Grbavica the beautiful fountain in Palma's summer garden stands out like a spring blossom. This is not just a café. It's a relic of old Sarajevo.

Ramis Sarači (old town, along the main Ferhadija walkway); tel: 033 535 947. Probably the most famous of all the sweet shops in town. The amount of traffic that goes through there amazes me. The cakes and sweets are mostly traditional and are a bargain for the low price of 1-2KM each.

Planeta Bravadžiluk bb (old town); tel: 033 447 447. Not only a great place for sweets and strong espresso, but also a perfect place for people watching.

Imperijal Titova (centre; by the eternal flame); tel: 033 210 699. Immediately after the war, Imperijal's owner placed a Christmas tree in his shop window to show the world that this city continued to be a multi-ethnic one. Sarajevo held its breath: would this not lead to violence? It did not, and the point had been made: minorities could live here without having to hide their traditions. This is a great place to sit in. It has great cakes and a wide variety of ice-cream. The crowds got too big to serve from within the shop so they moved their ice-cream to the front window. Single cones are only half a mark and the scoops are generous.

Internet café's

Internet Club 'Click' Kundurdžiluk 1 (old town); tel: 033 236 914. Nice staff and they've at least attempted to make a no-smoking area. It's not entirely smoke free but most likely they're the only ones in town to ever try it.

Internet Centre Ferhadija 21 (centre); 033 534 116. They charge the standard 1KM per hour and the connections are pretty good. They serve soft drinks and speak English.

so.ba Arts Academy (centre); 033 210 369. Upstairs are five or six computers with decent connections. There is always music pumping in the place and artsy folk smoking lots of cigarettes. If you're looking for a hip atmosphere to write to your friends and family or surf the net, this is your place.

FESTIVALS

The people in Bosnia and Herzegovina see plenty of opportunities for celebrations, festivals and annual traditions all year around. Close to Mostar, they feel that the strawberry season should start with a celebration. In Oštra Luka, they have an annual bull-fight. There are hundreds of other festivals, big and small. This section only lists the main festivals in Sarajevo. Check at the tourist office if there are any other festivals going on when you're around. Even if there are no festivals when you are in town, there are probably music, theatre and dance performances in the Kamerni Theatre, the National Theatre, and elsewhere.

Sarajevan Winter (February/March)
www.sarajevskazima.ba

This festival is the longest of all the Sarajevo festivals. Lasting for a full two months and with at least one thing on the agenda daily, this is a festival that includes many genres of art. There are all sorts of music, dance and theatre, of course, but there are also things like organised trips to the museum and city walks. This festival, as many other, showed the artistic resilience of the Sarajevans during the war: without interruptions, the festival was organised every single year.

Baščaršija Nights (July)
www.bascarsijskenoci.ba/kontakt_eng.htm

In the summer months, Sarajevo's old Turkish quarter is a most delightful place to be. Thousands of people are sipping their drinks or strolling about, and the atmosphere is completely laid back. In July, this part of town gets even better. Throughout the month, 'Baščaršija Nights' offers a programme full of folk dancing, opera, ballet, rock, love songs and poetry. There are art exhibitions and children programmes. The centre of the festival is located opposite the old town hall, but most activities take place in the open and are entirely free of charge. Posters and leaflets announce the programme well in advance.

International Folklore Festival (July)
www.sarajevoarts.ba/festivalfolklora_eng.html

Taking place in the second half of July, this festival overlaps with Baščaršija Nights. In the course of one week, folk groups come from all over the wider region to perform in Sarajevo. Sometimes they parade together, and you will see literally hundreds of men and women wearing their respective traditional costumes. It is nice, and shows how much these folk traditions are still alive in this part of the world.

Sarajevo Film Festival (August)
www.sff.ba/10SFF/program/eng/

This festival started in the last year of war, almost as an act of resistance. 'Look at us: you can't kill our spirit.' It showed 37 films in that year, many of them in simple VHS format and all sold out. The festival has changed enormously since then. Nowadays, the festival shows over 150 films on several locations and, obviously, no longer in VHS format. The movies are carefully selected, but together form an odd bunch of documentaries, regional movies, and films from all other parts of the world. They even have a children's program and the occassional mainstream Hollywood productions. The festival is immensely popular, and tickets are frequently sold out.

Sarajevo Film Festival, *by Babeth Knol*

If you come to Sarajevo in August you will feel a special atmosphere, even though a lot of domestic people are not in the city because of their holidays. The positive energy is caused by Sarajevo Film Festival, which is the main film festival in South-Eastern Europe.

Everything started in 1995 when director Mirsad Purivatra, who is also a professor at the film academy, decided to organise a film festival to get some film tapes back to Sarajevo. Directors came through the tunnel near the airport and over the mountains just to get their films into the city, and with the help of his wife, friends and colleagues he managed to make the first edition of Sarajevo Film Festival a fact.

Now, ten years later, the festival has grown out to be the biggest festival in South-Eastern Europe, and one of the top 10 festivals in Europe. Instead of it being organised by a couple of friends, there are 10 professionals working on it all year long, and during the festivals there are about 400 employees. It has grown to be one of the main cultural events of the year. There are 370 accredited journalists in town, (according to the spokesperson from SFF, this is almost as much as there were at the Olympic Games in 1984) and the festival's rapid growth is reflected in the number of festival guests. In 2003, the number was 500. In 2004, there were 700 guests.

Talking to Asja, the spokesperson of SFF (on the festival terrace that was filled with people at 9.45 in the morning), I asked her to tell me the secret of the success of Sarajevo Film Festival. With a big smile she told me that the main reason was that they had a great team, an inspiring director and a great love for the art of film. As a starting festival in a post-war period, a lot of promoting and inviting had to be done. They promised themselves to never be satisfied with the festival as it is, but take little steps of improvement every year.

For this jubilee year, a lot of little steps are taken. For the first time, there is a special programme for teenagers and children, the first in South-Eastern Europe. For the first time, SFF is licensed by FIAPF, The Federation of Film Producers, for its regional programme (Sarajevo has the largest number of regional productions). The regional aspect has become a lot more important, that is why there is a regional tribute program next to the international tribute screenings. It is the first time the Katrin Cartlidge Foundation Scholarship will be awarded to a promising filmmaker. This year, the scholarship is going to Greg Hall, director of 'The Plague'. And, a very special step forward, the award called 'Heart of Sarajevo' will be presented to the winner of the regional program for the first time.

This award is designed by a special friend of the Sarajevo Film

Festival, the famous French designer Agnes B. She was struck by the war in Bosnia and Herzegovina, and was organizing peace demonstrations in France. When she read in a newspaper about the plan for a film festival in Sarajevo, she was touched and wanted to do something to show her support. Therefore, she cut a heart out of the newspaper she was reading and sent it to Mirsad Purivatra. This heart is the first design of the Heart of Bosnia award, which is now made of metal instead of newspaper but still has the raff edges from the hasty use of the scissors.

People who want to see a movie at the festival do not have to stand in line for hours anymore. This year, the festival borrowed the computer system of Rotterdam Film Festival to distribute the tickets better. You can buy tickets in pre-sale by phone, at the box office during the festival and just before the movie starts. Tickets for the opening ceremony and the prime time screenings (20.30 h) are still very hard to get, but there are plenty of other great movies to see for the price of only 3-5KM (1,5-2,5 Euro).

The prices are amazingly affordable, thanks to the many sponsors such as BH Telecom. The best thing about this festival though is that you get to walk on the same red carpet as people like John Malkovich, Gerard Depardieu, Coolio, and Carol Bouquet. It is a pity that the press standing on the side is preparing their cameras rather than following you, but you just have to imagine that yourself.

European Literary Encounters (September)
www.malraux.ba (in the local language and French only, at the time of printing).

This annual gathering has guiding themes like 'Our Europe' or 'The future of the book in Europe', but the activities sometimes wander rather widely from that theme. Reporters, directors, writers, poets, actors, philosophers and translators from the wider region (all the way to North Africa) gather and spend a week talking about their experiences and ideas. These 'encounters' are a whole lot quieter than the music, film and theatre festivals, but its buzzing, informal series of gatherings is certainly very worthwhile for its special-interest audience. There is simultaneous interpretation and it is free of charge.

Teatar Fest (September)
www.tf.com.ba

This festival shows experimental projects, researches the 'directing, performing, speech, movements, costumes, music and other important elements of the theatre expressions' and presents 'projects which research new spaces, visions and media' (quotes taken from their website). In addition to showing theatre performances, there is lots of talking at this festival, and interested amateurs can watch movies, attend seminars and participate in workshops – all related to experimental theatre.

MESS (October)
www.mess.ba

MESS stands for 'male eksperimentalne scene', 'Small Experimental

Stage'. It is a theatre festival with a history of over a century. Theatre and modern dance performances are selected from all over Europe. The plays are performed in their original languages, sometimes with local language translation displayed above the stage. Theatre lovers who speak neither will still have a good time: most performances are very abstract and the language spoken is often of little importance. Be quick, as most performances are very well-visited. In 2005 and beyond, it will probably be possible to get your tickets online.

Sarajevo Fashion Week (November)
www.fashionweek.ba

This is all you'd expect from an international fashion week. In addition, there are local touches such as an opening show in which actors and singers wear handmade Bosnian fashion, and a closing show in which the best dressed public figures in Bosnia and Herzegovina receive fashion awards. It's possible to buy tickets for these and all other shows, but you have to be quick, as most seats are taken by invitees.

Jazz Festival (November)
www.jazzfest.ba

Having started in 1997, this is a relatively young festival. Somehow, it does not seem very 'Sarajevo'. The groups playing are rarely from the region – instead, they tend to come from Western Europe and North America – and the sponsor, as always when it comes to jazz festivals, is Dutch beer brewer Heineken. But it is popular, the groups rock, and the smoky places the groups perform in are invariably crowded.

International Music Festival - Jazz Fest
Sarajevo, by Amina Omićević (Thank you Damir Opalka)

Jazz in Southeastern Europe? Maybe. Jazz in the Balkans? Hardly. Jazz in Bosnia and Herzegovina? None. Wrong answers! Even if this area of the world might not seem as an attractive destination for a quality jazz audience, Sarajevo becomes a jazz-heart of Europe during the first week of November each year. Jazz Fest Sarajevo is an international, independent and non-profit attraction that has been organized annually since 1997. Through the years, it has developed into a respectable institution of jazz culture, featuring musicians from all over the world. Its genres vary from classical jazz to the modern ethno, fusion and lots of other interesting mixtures of styles and techniques. You can find the history of participants and contact details at www.jazzfest.ba.

Some of artists that performed at the Fest so far are Joe Zawinul Syndicate, Django Bates Quiet Nights, Richard Galliano Trio, Markus Stockhausen, Dhafer Youssef, Arild Andersen, Jiri Stivin, Ali Haurand, Vienna Art Orchestra, Irene Schweizer, Christy Doran's New Bag, Karl Ratzer, Bodan Arsovski & Ezgija Orchestra and Vlatko Stefanovski.

As it's getting better year by year, the 7th Jazz Fest Sarajevo of 2003 is a great example for an overview of the Fest's contents and atmosphere. On the opening night the British tenor saxophonist Denys Baptiste performed with a great band of multinational musicians a tribute to Martin Luther King (Let Freedom

Ring!) as continuous fusion jazz with Afro and gospel elements. The afterparty in Coloseum followed, with the classical jazz repertoire of the fifties played by the local Marko Đorđević Minority. The second night performed "the greatest refreshment of the Fest" – the dynamic Esbjorn Svennson Trio (E. S. T.). They played an interesting combination of jazz with downtemp and drum'n'bass and experimented with contrabass and piano effects, nicely spiced up with an unusual set of percussions. Even if it's not a right measure of quality, it might be interesting to mention that E. S. T. was one of the first jazz performers broadcasted by MTV. On later nights came Soweto Kinch 4tet with Abram Wilson who combined hip-hop with traditional jazz, Dhafer Youssef with his compositions made out of traditional Sufi music, electronic sounds and jazz, Nenad Vasilić Balkan trio that played established folk songs through a jazz tune... And then the greatest star of the Fest went out on the stage – the soul diva from Great Britain, Juliet Roberts – and left the audience breathless. So did many other musicians that performed in Sarajevo during those five days of the Fest. The atmosphere in the city was just... jazzy!

Perhaps the only complaint about the Fest could be the locations where the concerts have been played at. Bigger bands perform at Dom policije but it's often the case that there are more visitors (sold tickets) than the number of seats. Afterparties, smaller concerts and sessions are played usually at different jazz clubs or at Coloseum, a casino that is always crowded and definitely not a place where the beauty of jazz comes out in full (though phenomenal performers such as Geraldo Nunez Group with the flamenco dancer Carmen Cortez sounded great even here). Coming festivals will certainly bring us some changes in the choice of concert halls and clubs.

During the seven years of its existence, Jazz Fest Sarajevo proved to be an important international festival of jazz and its derivates. It is worthwhile being in Sarajevo in the beginning of November – you will get a warm welcome, great music for a very affordable price and interesting, spontaneous jam sessions all over.

What more do you need if you are in love with all that jazz?!

MAPA SARAJEVO U KOLORU

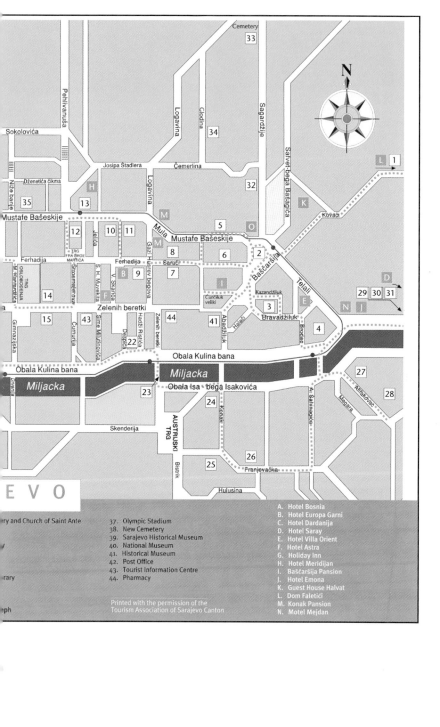

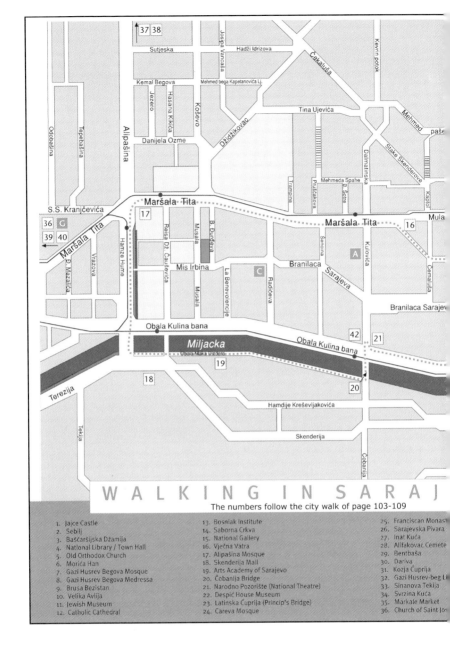

W A L K I N G   I N   S A R A J

The numbers follow the city walk of page 103-109

1. Jajce Castle
2. Sebilj
3. Baščaršijska Džamija
4. National Library / Town Hall
5. Old Orthodox Church
6. Morića Han
7. Gazi Husrev Begova Mosque
8. Gazi Husrev Begova Medressa
9. Brusa Bezistan
10. Velika Avlija
11. Jewish Museum
12. Catholic Cathedral

13. Bosniak Institute
14. Saborna Crkva
15. National Gallery
16. Vječna Vatra
17. Alipašina Mosque
18. Skenderija Mall
19. Arts Academy of Sarajevo
20. Čobanija Bridge
21. Narodno Pozorište (National Theatre)
22. Despić House Museum
23. Latinska Ćuprija (Princip's Bridge)
24. Careva Mosque

25. Franciscan Monast
26. Sarajevska Pivara
27. Inat Kuća
28. Alifakovac Cemete
29. Bentbaša
30. Dariva
31. Kozja Ćuprija
32. Gazi Husrev-beg Li
33. Sinanova Tekija
34. Svrzina Kuća
35. Markale Market
36. Church of Saint Jos

WALKING IN SARAJEVO

Though there are numerous interesting areas to walk in the city, most of any walking tour through Sarajevo centres around the old town Turkish quarters and Marijin Dvor, both of which are situated in the flat valley of the Miljacka River.

There are a few sites, however, that require a considerable uphill walk. The old narrow streets on both sides of the river above Baščaršija are well worth the wander but if you are not up for the steep trek to places like **Jajce Castle** (Eugene of Savoy Castle) and the ruins of the medieval town, there are local buses and car tours. The views of the whole city from these areas (comprising Vratnik to the north side of the old town and Bistrik to the south) are spectacular.

Otherwise a walking tour of the main sites can be done in about three hours depending on your pace and number of café stops. There are several city guides but the best of the certified guides can be found via the Tourist Information Centre or through City Tour. The latter offers professionally guided tours in all major European languages and even in Swedish, Dutch and Czech. Group tours cost 80-120 KM.

If you opt to see Jajce Castle and the ruins of the medieval city, it's probably wisest to start in the hilly area stretching north to east of the old town. Local bus number 51 to Vratnik leaves hourly from the main taxi, bus and tram station in **Baščaršija** near **Sebilj.** You know you've arrived at the medieval fort when you reach the second large, arched gate. Going straight ahead will lead you through the gate and going right will lead to the fort.

From there it's all downhill and a very nice walk through the ambient backstreets of Sarajevo's oldest quarters leading to Baščaršija. This was the centre of life during the Ottoman rule from the 1440s until the empire collapsed in 1878. Much of its oriental flavour has been preserved. It is famous for craftsmen of every kind who still hammer away at authentic handmade goods as their forefathers did centuries ago.

The heart of Baščaršija, **Sebilj Square**, is the famous pigeon square where the main public fountain is located. This is a perfect place to rest a little and have your first of many coffees. The Bosnian governor under the Ottomans, *Hadži Mehmed-paša Kukavica*, built the first **fountain** on Baščaršija in 1753. The fountain was relocated to its present location in 1891 by the architect *Aleksandar Vitek* who modelled it on Moorish style, copied from the stone sebilj in Constantinopole.

The coffee and sweet shops near Sebilj all serve Turkish coffee with the jellied sweet rahatlokum. For the best (and, with heavy cream and chocolate sauce, weirdest) cappuccino, go to café Tunel, situated right next to the fountain.

Just outside the square is **Kazandžiluk Street**, the famous copper-smith trading place on the east side of Baščaršija. Here you'll find great antiques, hand-carved copper dishes and oriental decor. It may seem strange to find shell cartridges left over from the war on sale here but as Sarajevo was pounded by over one million projectiles during its 1,400 day siege, it occurred to the ever resourceful coppersmiths that the most practical use of the enormous quantity of left-over casings and cartridges was to hand-carve beautiful designs on them and sell them to tourists.

Make sure to bargain with the friendly vendors and ask specifically if the item of interest is handmade by the craftsmen or imported from Turkey

- they sell both. Next to Kazandžiluk Street is **Baščaršijska džamija** or the marketplace mosque. Its official name is Džamija Havadže Duraka (Havadja Durak's mosque) and it was built in the 1530s. This mosque often has the imam (local Muslim priest) sing the call to prayer from the minaret. Its mystical sounds resonate throughout the čaršija.

Not far from Sebilj on the bank of the Miljacka River is the **National Library** built during Austrian rule in Bosnia and Herzegovina. Originally used as the Town Hall, this building, like Sebilj, was designed by Aleksandar Vitek, who also began construction of it in 1892. Following Vitek's death in 1894, it was completed in 1895 with the design supplemented by *Ćiril Iveković*.

Exactly 100 years after construction began, centuries of history went up in flames when Serbian forces deliberately targeted the National Library with incendiary grenades in the early days of the Sarajevo siege. Everything was lost, due in no small part to the fact that the besieging forces directed mortar and machine gun fire at every entrance of the building while fire-fighters tried to douse the flames and citizens of Sarajevo attempted to rescue the books. (Another fire that summer destroyed Sarajevo's Oriental Institute along with its entire inventory of books.)

"All over the city sheets of burned paper, fragile pages of grey ashes, floated down like a dirty black snow. Catching a page you could feel its heat, and for a moment read a fragment of text in a strange kind of black and gray negative, until, as the heat dissipated, the page melted to dust in your hand." (Dr. Kemal Bakaršić, librarian of Bosnia's National Museum, describing the burning of the National and University Library, 25-27 August 1992).

The building is still under reconstruction. Upon completion, it will once again be one of the most beautiful buildings in the entire country.

Only a few hundred metres away, doubling back across the Sebilj Square, and following the one-way system on Mula-Mustafe Bašeskije street is the **Old Orthodox Church**, often referred to as simply the old church. It is estimated that the church was built in 1539/40. The Orthodox Church grew considerably in Bosnia from this point on. The church caught fire several times. The turret by the church had a dome until the first half of the 20th century. Following the reconstruction by architect *Dušan Smiljanić*, this turret took on the simple form it has today. The museum has many icons and frescos from that era as well as even earlier relics brought to Sarajevo from other Orthodox lands. The museum was arranged by Jeftan Despić, the sexton of the old church.

Ferhadija walkway (referred to still by many Sarajevans by its old name, 'Vase Miskina') is perhaps the most charming part of town. It stretches from Sebilj in the heart of Baščaršija all the way to the eternal flame in the city centre. Ferhadija is almost always filled with locals strolling through town, window shopping, chatting or just enjoying the pleasant energy of walking up and down.

Along the Ferhadija, still in Baščaršija, is **Morića han**. It was known as a caravansaray, meaning 'castle of the caravans'. The function of the han was to provide warehouse space, stables and accommodation for traders coming from near and far. It got its name from the inn operator Mustafa Morić.

In the 1970s it was renovated and restored as a tourist attraction and in 1985 it was adapted into a complex of several restaurants and café's, which along with an oriental rug shop and office spaces on the first floor where the inn rooms used to be, are what it features today. It's a lovely place to sit and have a drink in the courtyard, while losing track of time. And despite its various renovations and adaptations, it is not too difficult to imagine how it used to be.

Gazi Husrev-begova Mosque on Ferhadija, a very short distance from Morića Han, is the most significant Islamic object in Bosnia and Herzegovina. It is perhaps the finest example of Ottoman Islamic architecture on the Balkan Peninsula. The Persian architect, *Adžem Esir Ali*, was the leading architect of his time within the empire. The mosque's design favours the early Istanbul mosque style. The original structure was built in 1530 but was largely destroyed when Eugene of Savoy plundered Sarajevo in 1697. It was fully restored by 1762 but was destroyed again in 1879. The last full-scale reconstruction of Gazi Husrev-begova Mosque was in 1886. Although it was damaged during the last conflict, most of its precious original oriental design survived unscathed. It is open to visitors at certain times of the day. It is important to stay to the side during prayer time; it is the main mosque in the city and is usually filled by local worshippers. Directly across the stone walkway is the **Gazi Husrev-beg Medressa**. A medressa is an Islamic educational institution. It was founded on January 8 1537. The medressa is situated in **Sarači Street** which is simply an extension of the Ferhadija walkway.

At the end of the marble-like walkway in the old quarters is the **Brusabezistan.** This beautiful oriental department store, with a long corridor topped by six domes, was the main trade centre for silk from Bursa in Asia Minor. Masons from Dubrovnik helped build the structure designed by *Grand Vizier Rustem-paša* in 1551. After having been heavily damaged during the shelling of Sarajevo, Bezistan is once again a trade centre lined with tiny boutiques, café's and souvenir shops. It's definitely worth a browse.

From the front entrance to Brusa-bezistan, you shouldn't fail to notice a clock-tower extending up from between the old buildings. Built in the 17th century to ensure punctual attendance at daily prayers, it was destroyed along with the Gazi Husrev-begova Mosque in 1697 and, like the mosque, fully restored again in 1762. The Austro-Hungarians added upper floors to the tower and the clock and mechanisms brought from London by Sarajevan traders.

Through a small passageway between Ferhadija and Bašeskija streets is the **Velika avlija** (Grand Yard), also known as the Jewish quarters. The **Jewish Museum** (033 535 589) is located here. The Sephardic Jews who settled in Sarajevo quickly established themselves as tradesmen within the Ottoman Empire. The first temple to be built was the **Stari hram** in 1581, less then a century after the Jews were expelled from Spain. The old synagogue, or Il Kal Grandi, was also destroyed in 1697 and again in 1788.

As the Jewish community continued to grow there were calls to build a larger place of worship and the old temple was expanded in 1821. The upper floors were used by the women and the ground floor by men - the same tradition is practised by Muslims. You can arrange a tour of the Old Jewish Synagogue by calling the Despić House Museum (033 215 531).

A short walk out of the Turkish quarters and you'll find yourself in the part of Ferhadija that resembles the centre of Vienna instead of Istanbul. The walk down Ferhadija street literally takes you through Sarajevo's past. Religious harmony has always been the backbone of Sarajevo's multi-ethnic community. The **Catholic cathedral** was completed in 1889 when the Austrians had gained full control of the city. It falls under the metropolitan of the Vrhbosna archbishop and is dedicated to the Most Holy Heart of Jesus. The cathedral was designed by the architect *Noble Josip Vancaš* in the neo-Gothic style, with some elements of Romanesque. It is very similar to the Notre Dame Cathedral in Dijon. The Pope led mass here during his visit in 1997. The cathedral is usually open for visitors. Don't be surprised to find Sarajevo's youth hanging out on the steps of the cathedral; it has always been a popular (and central) place to hang out or wait for a friend.

Behind the cathedral near the music school is the **Bosniak Institute**. The institute is dedicated to the history of the Bosnian Muslims, or Bosniacs. It's an interesting place to see old documents and read about famous Muslim writers and historians, and it offers an interesting insight into the national identity of the Bosnian Muslims.

Following Ferhadija to **Trg Oslobođenja**, or Liberation Square, (also known widely as 'Park Svjetlost', named after a large book publishing house with premises on the square) is the **Saborna crkva**. This is the largest Orthodox church in Sarajevo. Dedicated to the Most Holy Mother of God, its builder and architect was the well-known Andrija Damjanov. The church is an example of a mixture of baroque and Byzantine-Serb style. The church was consecrated on St Elijah's Day, on August 2 1872. The construction of the church was supported by the Ottoman Sultan Abdul-Aziz and the Russian czar's family. The great icon on the north wall of the church was painted by *Paja Jovanović*. It is open to visitors most days.

Across the street from the orthodox church is the **National Gallery of Bosnia and Herzegovina** (Zelenih beretki 8). In this gallery, the work of the famous icon painter *Tudor Vuković Desisalić* is displayed, as well as work of most other great past and present artists from Bosnia and Herzegovina.

Jumping back on to Ferhadija and continuing west takes you to the end of this charming walkway. You may see several holes in the pavement filled with something like red candle wax. These commemorate massacre sites from the siege and are dubbed 'Sarajevo roses'. In some cases, there are plaques on the wall describing the incident. The victims were always civilians waiting in line for bread, water or food.

As Ferhadija meets Tito Street the **Vječna vatra** (Eternal Flame) burns in memory of the Serbs, Croats, Muslims and other partisans who gave their lives in the liberation of Sarajevo from the fascists in the Second World War.

It is nice to explore all the little side streets off Ferhadija. It will be hard not to find something that grabs your interest. There are plenty of other sites to see and, with the small tourist maps distributed for free at the Tourist Information Centre, it should be easy to find most of them.

Alipašina Mosque, on the corner of Tito Street and Ali-pašina Street, was one of the most dangerous spots during the war. Hastily made barricades comprising bombed buses and cargo containers were positioned across the wide junction at the edge of the mosque to block the view of snipers. The Ali-pašina endowment was built in 1560/61 by the Bosnian governor *Ali-paša* and it is renowned as the most harmonious mosque in Sarajevo. The architect was a scholar of Sinan, a master builder within the empire. Ali-pašina Mosque is located along the koševski stream, very close to the Sarajevo town hall building. The tombstones on the corner of the property are the graves of *Avdo Sumbul and Behdžet Mutavelić*, fighters against the Austro-Hungarian army.

Across the Miljacka River is the **Skenderija Mall**. This was built as the media centre for the 1984 Olympics and has been transformed into a shopping centre with modern shops and styles. On the bottom floor of Skenderija is the **Museum of Contemporary Art** (033 201 208). There are frequent expositions of international and local artists. Next to the museum is the **Collegium Artisticum Art Gallery**. It's more of a place where the older intellectual corps gather. There is always a small exhibition on the walls and you can find out information on cultural events inside.

The pedestrian path on the south side of the Miljacka leads to the only evangelist church in Bosnia and Herzegovina. It was built in the last years of the 19th century. The structure, however, is no longer a church. The building was donated to the city and turned into the **Arts Academy of Sarajevo.** Feel free to have a wander. There is a café and internet club inside. The end of the pedestrian path takes you to **Čobanija Bridge**. Crossing back over the river you will find the main post office. This Viennese structure is one of the finest examples of Austrian architecture in town. The inside has been completely renovated and is well worth a peek.

Next to the post office is the **Narodno pozorište** or National Theatre, built in 1899 by the architect of the evangelist church and representing the neo-Renaissance style. Walking east from the theatre along the Miljacka, you will pass by the **Despić House Museum**, a Serbian tradesmen house from Ottoman times that is preserved in its original form. Opposite the Despić House Museum, there is the **Latinska ćuprija**, which is also still referred to as Principov most ('Princip's Bridge') as it was here that *Archduke Ferdinand* and his pregnant wife were shot and killed on St Vitus Day, June 28 1914 by Gavrilo Princip. It was this event that caused Austria to declare war on Serbia, mother Russia came to the rescue and declared war on Austria and World War I soon followed. Sarajevo gets the unfair label of starting WWI. All the elements for WWI were in place – once again the struggle for the Balkan Peninsula after the fall of the Ottoman Empire – and this was simply the spark to put the forces long at work into action. Despite being remembered mostly for this tragic event, the bridge itself is quite a remarkable example of Ottoman bridge building. It was first built in 1541 as a wooden structure. A stone bridge was built by *Ali Ajnibeg* in 1565. Flooding seriously damaged the new stone bridge at the end of the 18th century and was reconstructed by Hadži Abdulah Briga in 1798. In Ottoman times its official name was Frenkluk ćuprija, named after the neighbouring Catholic quarter in **Bistrik.** A monument to Archduke Franz Ferdinand and Sofia Hotek was built in 1917 near the bridge, only to be demolished in 1918. The name 'Princip's Bridge' was unofficially introduced after 1918. In 1993 the bridge was renamed Latinska ćuprija.

By crossing the Latinska Ćuprija you enter the **Bistrik** district of the old town. The park along the river is a favourite gathering spot during the summer. Its tree-covered green space provides a cool and pleasant break from the hot summer days. Up river is the **Careva Mosque**. The original mosque was built in 1457 as a gift for Sultan Mehmed II. It was built by *Isa-beg Ishaković* who also built the famous castle Saraj, after which Sarajevo was named. The present-day mosque was built in 1566 by order of Sulejman the Great. Past Careva Mosque up **Konak Street** is the **Franciscan Monastery and Church of St Ante**, in the old Catholic quarters of Bistrik. It is now run by a monk name *Fra Ivo* – he is also one of the leading figures in

Bosnia and Herzegovina for religious reconciliation. He speaks pretty good English and is a wonderfully friendly man. If you run in to him, I'm willing to bet he'll have time for a chat. He has a wealth of knowledge about Bosnian history and certainly represents the multi-ethnic, multi-confessional spirit of the city. The monastery and church were built during the Austro-Hungarian period. The church holds many ancient artefacts and documents in the old bosančica script. Across the street is the **Sarajevska pivara** (brewery). It is not accessible for guests but the brewery played a great role in the survival of the city during the siege. It is built on top of one of the largest fresh water springs in the city. With all water cut off this became the only source of clean drinking water for thousands of Sarajevans. It's no wonder that Sarajevo beer is by far the favourite! They have recently opened a new **pivnica** (brewery bar and restaurant) that serves the only dark beer made in Sarajevo on tap. It may seem a bit fancy – but the beer is great, the prices are low and it has a great atmosphere in the evenings.

Take a wander through some of the side streets before heading back down towards the river. You should come out near **Inat kuća** which is one of the finest traditional restaurants in town, situated in a house that was originally built on the other side of the river.

Passing Inat kuća to the right is **Alifakovac** Street. Alifakovac is the eastern quarter of old Sarajevo. Its original name was believed to have been chosen after Ali Ufak (Alija the Short), a legendary sheikh who was buried at the Alifakovac graveyard. In fact the origin of this name is in honour of *Ali Fakit,* a scientist from Sarajevo from the first half of the 15th century who was mentioned in Gazi Husrev-beg's foundation from 1462.

The Alifakovac graveyard is a final resting place for Muslim foreigners who died and were buried in Sarajevo. The cemetery is interesting not only from a historical viewpoint but also for the great view of the old town it offers.

On the other side of the graveyard is a walkway leading to a wooden footbridge that crosses the Miljacka. **Bentbaša** is the canyon area along the river. There is a public pool and a bit further on is a long footpath used by joggers, walkers and bikers. It is closed to vehicles and is a wonderful place to take a peaceful walk along the river (which cleans up considerably after leaving the old town). Along the footpath is also an open-air climbing area called **Dariva.** Dariva is a favourite local climbing spot with pre-marked paths for both free climbing and bouldering. If you're up for an even longer walk, further east in the canyon is the **Kozja ćuprija** or Goats Bridge (and a traditional restaurant with terrace right next to it). It is an elegant stone bridge (over 10m high). According to the travel journals of Katrin Zen, the bridge existed before 1550. Bosnian viziers were welcomed at Kozja ćuprija and it is here that the pilgrims to Mecca began their long journey east.

On the north side of the old town are many of the Islamic institutions built by or dedicated to Gazi Husrev-beg. Heading up Sagrdžije Street is the **Gazi Husrev-beg Library**, the most important institution of its kind in the Balkans. It was founded in 1537 by the Bosnian governor and benefactor. It now contains over 50,000 manuscripts and books. The library is open to the public. Further up the hill is **Sinanova tekija** (dervish house) of the Kaderija dervish order. Here the mystical order chants prayers intended to move them into a trance. It seems that the tekija was constructed by Hadži Sinan-aga, a rich merchant from Sarajevo. Otherwise, it is possible that his son Mustafa-paša Silahdar built the tekija in honour of his father. To get a look at an authentic Ottoman house from the 18th century pay a visit to the **Svrzina kuća** (Svrzo's House). This house/museum is a great example of a wealthy beg's house. The house is located on Glodžina 8 Street that runs parallel with Logavina Street. The high walls around the garden mark the intimate and secret life of the wealthier begs. The balconies are made of intricately carved wood and the large sitting rooms are typical of Ottoman homes created to receive a large extended family. The house has been well restored and guided tours through the house are possible throughout the week.

Towards the end of the conflict, on August 28 1995, in Bosnia and Herzegovina, the **Markale** market on Mula-Mustafe Bašeskije was bombed by the Bosnian Serbs. Although today it is a bustling market it was this massacre that killed dozens of civilians and convinced NATO to finally intervene militarily to end the siege of the city. Within months of these events all parties were at the peace table and the Dayton Accords were signed soon after.

Travelling west, Maršala Tita Street turns into Zmaja od Bosne in the centre of the Marijin Dvor quarter, which itself was the end of urban Sarajevo until modern times. At the junction near the twin towers (a very small version of the former New York skyscrapers) is the **Church of Saint Joseph**. This Catholic building is the work of Karl Parzika. The large bombed-out building across the street was the parliament building. It was in this square in early 1992 that tens of thousands of Sarajevans of all ethnicities took to the streets to say no to war

If by chance you find yourself on the north end of town by the **Olympic Stadium** with the copper roof, notice the endless rows of new white tombstones. The **new cemetery** on both sides of Patriotske lige Street holds the graves of victims of the longest siege in modern European history. It's a startling reminder of the immense number of people killed there.

MUSEUMS

- **National Museum**

Address: Zmaja od Bosne 7

Working hours: from Tuesday to Friday and on Sunday, from 10.00 to 14.00

Entrance fee: 5 KM

This museum, like most other things in Sarajevo, came out of the war looking battered. But its exterior has been renovated recently, and it has been a job well done: these four Austro-Hungarian buildings do not look their age (120 years) and would make this museum worth visiting even without any exhlblts.

After having seen the exterior, the museum entrance is a bit discouraging - but they're working on that too. The halls on the right show archaeological findings: jewellery, weapons, mosaics and examples of ancient scripts, among other things. The explanations are good and make the exhibits a lot more interesting, but they are printed in the local language only. By far the most interesting item is exhibited in the small room on the first floor: the Sarajevo Haggadah. This 14th century Spanish-Jewish book shows pictures of people and portrays the world as being round – both highly unusual at the time. It was taken from Spain to Sarajevo in 1492, disappeared, and reappeared in 1894 when a young boy brought it to the

Sarajevo museum. It was hidden by a Moslem scholar to escape the Holocaust and, in this recent war, taken from the Sarajevo library just weeks before that library went up in flames. It disappeared once more - the rumour was that the Bosniacs had sold it in order to buy weapons – and resurfaced when the Bosnian President displayed it briefly in 1995. Now, 700 years after it was hand-written, it is on permanent display in a climate-controlled room in this museum. Don't bump your head against the glass window that prevents visitors from entering the room: you almost can't see the glass is there.

In between the four building is the botanic garden with its stećci. It is a quiet place with benches. If the museum's opening hours hadn't been so weird (and if there had been a small cafeteria), you could sit here for hours.

The ethnographic exhibition on display in the building on the left is the only part of the museum with good English-language explanations. It tastefully shows all that you would expect from an ethnographic museum, as well as a life-size replica of a rich Ottoman era family house.

• Sarajevo Historical Museum

Address: Brusa-bezistan, Abadžiluk (100 metres from the square with the pigeons)

Opening hours at the time of writing: from Tuesday to Saturday: 10.00 – 17.00; Sunday from 10.00 to 13.00; Monday closed. Some time in 2005, the museum will probably close its doors on Sundays and be open on Mondays from 10.00 to 17.00.

Entry fee: 2 KM.

This museum opened in October 2004. It is situated right in the centre of town, in a beautiful six-dome Ottoman building. The collection – costumes, coins, tombstones and other items you would expect to find in a historical museum – is tastefully exhibited and accompanied with interesting texts in excellent English. The museum's centre piece is a scale model of the entire old town. Some city guides have included this museum in their tours.

• Svrzo's House (Svrzina kuća)

Address: Glodina 8

Opening hours: from Tuesday to Saturday from 10.00 to 17.00; on Sunday from 10.00 to 13.00.

Entrance fee: 2 KM

This is an 18th century Ottoman house, beautifully restored and furnished. It is truly Ottoman, but has a distinct Bosnian feel to it. Your tour around the house is interesting if you do it by yourself, but will have even more value if you take a guided tour and listen to stories about the shower system, the furniture (or, in western eyes, lack thereof), the dining arrangements, the kitchen, the all-important privacy and, more in general, the dynamics of a wealthy family in Ottoman times.

• The Jewish Museum

Address: Mula-Mustafe Bašeskije; the building on the left at the square with the round flower beds, next to galleria Novi hram. Go through the really low iron door to get to the garden and the museum entrance.

Opening hours: from Monday to Friday and Sunday, from 10.00 to 17.00.

Entry fee: 2 KM

The arrival, lifestyle and treatment of the Jews that left Spain in the 16th century, and settled in and around Sarajevo, is told from the perspective of the Jewish community itself. The texts are in good English and the material is exhibited tastefully, using each of the three floors of this recently renovated cobble-stone building in the centre of town. The original Jewish spice shop that had been operational for 300 years before being closed down in 1942 is particularly nice. Enter the top floor only if you are up to Second World War photographs of genocide.

• The Old Orthodox Church and Museum

Address: Mula-Mustafe Bešeskije 59

Opening hours of the museum: daily, except on Mondays and Orthodox holidays, from 10.00 until 15.00. These hours are not always adhered to. The church is officially open every day from 08.00 until 17.00.

Entry fee: 3 KM for the museum. The church itself does not charge an entry fee.

If you don't pay attention, you will pass by this church without noticing it, as it is a modest building, separated from the street by a massive wall. The wall doesn't make this church look very welcoming from the outside, but does manage to keep out all the noise and seemingly even much of the pollution. Once inside, you are in an oasis of quietness and serenity.

This church was built on a previous church's foundations that date back to the sixth century. After a number of fires in the 17th and early 18th century, it was rebuilt in its current shape in 1730. It is a building of wonderful simplicity: square, dark, with two floors, and a very large iconostasis (a wooden screen with icons) covering the entire right hand wall.

In contrast, the museum is light and has a somewhat sterile ambiance. It features bibles, paintings, frescos, ceremonial ornaments and a few gowns, all from the period between the 15th and 18th century. The accompanying texts tell you what is on display, but nothing more.

• National Gallery

Address: Zelenih beretki 8

Opening hours: from Tuesday to Saturday, from 10.00 to 18.00.

Entrance free of charge.

The National Gallery has a permanent exhibition of both old and contemporary paintings and sculptures, all made by Bosnian artists. In addition, there are temporary exhibitions, differing widely in nature and quality. It is by far the best place to view the work of Bosnia and Herzegovina's most influential artists of the 20th century. In the ground floor gallery there are frequent modern exhibitions and the occasional soft jazz concerts.

• Museum of Contemporary Art (Ars Aevi)

Address: Centar Skenderija, Terezije bb

Opening hours: Monday to Friday from 9:00 to 16:00

This museum is unexpectedly located in the left corner of the rather dull Skenderija building. It's an experimental place with a small permanent collection and changing exhibitions that originate from all over Europe. Like several artistic venues in Sarajevo, financing is a problem and they are sometimes forced to close temporarily. Call before going: tel: 033 201 208

● Historical Museum

Address: Zmaja od Bosne 5

Working hours: from Tuesday to Friday from 09.00 to 14.00. On Saturday and Sunday from 09.00 to 13.00.

Entrance fee: 1 KM

The contrast with its beautiful Austro-Hungarian neighbour, in which the National Museum is housed, could not be more pronounced. The Historical Museum is housed in a small, war-damaged building. On the ground floor, this museum has two small exhibitions. The exhibition on the recent war is impressive simply because the 'fresh' topic makes it so, but otherwise lacks style, variety and content. The other exhibition is not more than a set of enlarged old photographs of people and nature. The upper part of this museum hosts a modern art exhibition. At the time of writing this exhibition was closed because its patron failed to pay the rent on time.

● Tunnel Museum

Address: Tuneli 1

Opening hours: every day from 09.00 to 17.00.

Entrance fee: 5 KM

From July 1993 until the end of the war, one narrow, 1.5 metre high and over 700-metre long tunnel was the lifeline for the besieged people in Sarajevo. It brought food and tools to town and wounded or otherwise vulnerable people to safety. It started in the garage of a house, went under the airport, and ended on the other side in the suburb of Dobrinja. Notwithstanding a few stories of war profiteering (thousands of desperate people going through a life-saving tunnel every day obviously has huge potential for that), this tunnel became the besieged city's symbol of resistance and survival.

By now, this tunnel has collapsed, and all that remains is a video with a lot of original tunnel footage, the first few tunnel metres, and a museum telling the story. At the time of writing, this is still an improvised and somewhat shabby museum, managed by the house's original inhabitants. A lot of people go here, but it can also be completely empty for hours on stretch. I find that amazing, and do not doubt that, within years, this place is one of the most important tourist magnets in the entire Balkan region. Until that time comes, this museum is a museum made by amateurs, a little hard to find, but really, really worth the search.

The dreary tunnel crossing

I sometimes forget a few things about crossing the tunnel during the height of the war. After visiting the museum I realised that it's difficult to get a real feel for what it was like to disappear into the earth in order to reach the besieged city. The tunnel was closed to internationals during the war and very few non-Bosnians ever crossed it. I did three times but not because I was someone special. VIPs were allowed to cross the airport with a UN tank escort. Working for a small (but effective) aid organisation I wasn't high on the UN's priority list. Luckily the work we did meant a lot more to the Bosnians, and thanks to their trust and help I can now tell you one story amongst thousands of the Sarajevo tunnel crossing.

Arriving at the tunnel after creeping down Mount Igman on a dark night with no lights was an unforgettable experience. The sounds of the hundreds of people waiting to pass through the tunnel was like the desperate murmur from some back alley filled with homeless people. Rubbish was strewn everywhere. Thin and pale people stood over small fires waiting for word that the tunnel crossing was open. Besides moving the human cargo that could carry a week's worth of food on its back, the tunnel was the only means for ammunition to reach the town. Small trolleys were built on rail bars to move ammunition and humanitarian aid back and forth. Artillery and small arms fire peppered the night and every few minutes a round would land in the vicinity ... I was the only one startled by the close calls. Waiting in circumstances like these gives a whole new meaning to the concept of time. The shaken but determined energy of the masses waiting to cross gave me a sort of silent courage and aroused my instincts of survival.

Badly wounded civilians and soldiers were sometimes carted through the passageway. We would often wait for hours for the long queue from the other side to file out like moles. I only crossed the tunnel at night, due to the treacherous road down Igman that constantly came under fire regardless of who or what you were. The chaos and buzzing energy that would grip the entire group when our side of the tunnel opened was intense to say the least. I always had to go with a military escort and I was forbidden to travel with a camera or any electrical devices. If I'm not mistaken we entered the tunnel through what resembled a kitchen. The maze of walls and trenches seemed to be intentionally designed to confuse. Once we entered, the air changed, the smell changed, the walls hugged our elbows and we literally had to bend in half to walk or waddle, through the 700m corridor. The iron reinforcements above dripped with moisture and the muddied floors were covered with wooden planks. We all banged our heads at least once.

A woman carrying a sack of potatoes which appeared to weigh more than me collapsed from exhaustion. My friend and colleague Skye Corbett, also an American aid worker, didn't hesitate to sling the sack on his back and carry it the rest of the way for the old woman. Sweat dripped from our foreheads and the muscles in our backs began to reject our unnatural position.

Exiting was as chaotic as entering. An even deeper maze of trenches wound its way through a field and into a flat in the suburbs of Dobrinja. Walls, sweat, sniper fire, dirt, mud, babies crying, men arguing and everyone chain smoking were just a few of the thousands of pictures my senses registered in those few minutes of clambering to safety. One journey was over and now the challenge of reaching town through the deadly sniper alleys was next on our agenda. In a nutshell, it went a little something like that.

ART GALLERIES, *by Heather Day*

The current situation for state-funded art in Bosnia and Herzegovina is a little unsure. The government under the direction of the High Representative Paddy Ashdown has cut spending on culture significantly. According to a gallery representative at the National Gallery, wages have plunged and will cease to exist in 3 months time. For the National Gallery this does not mean closure and exhibitions will continue via alternative funding.

Aside from the general selection of state and independent galleries there are a few small commercial but still artistically interesting galleries and other venues that exhibit artworks. They are all listed together here. This list is not exhaustive and there are other small galleries dotted round.

ALU

Obala Maka Dizdara 3; tel. 033/210 369; open: 10 – 18 hours (Sat and Sun closed); genre: all, new media, painting etc.

Collegium Artisticum

Terezije bb; tel. 033 270 752; open 10 – 18 hours (Sun closed); genre: photography, painting and graphic art.

Gabrijel

Maršala Tita 56/1; tel. 033 471 184; open 9 – 15 hours (Sat and Sun closed); genre: photos mainly (also host book promotions).

Bosanki Kulturni Centar

Branilaca Sarajeva 24; tel: 033 441 798.

IPC

Luledžina 12; tel. 033 232 954.

Java

Maršala Tita 7; open 11 – 19 hours weekdays, sat 10 – 17 hours; genre: commercial gallery with antiques, fashion items, pottery, sculpture and paintings for sale. You can pick up an original painting for about 50 Euros.

Mak

Sime Milutinovića Sarajlije 7; tel: 033 471 828; open 10 – 19 hours (Sat and Sun 10 – 15 hours); genre: paintings, all genres also book launches/promotions, theatre exhibitions, performance art.

National Library

Obala Kulina bana; while renovation takes place and the books are resting elsewhere the library has become a temporary gallery space. The building itself is an architectural masterpiece of pseudo Moorish design and the inside still has many interesting features; genre: currently installation/sculpture work.

Novi hram

Mula-Mustafe Bašeskije 38; tel: 033 233 280; this building was originally a synagogue. It was given to the community as a present so that it could become a gallery space; genre - all.

Paleta

Hamdije Kreševljakovića 13; tel: 033 532 655; open: 19 – 23 hours.

Preporod

Mula Mustafa Bašeskije 63; tel: 033 445 196; e-mail: 033 445 196; genre: this commercial gallery houses work by local and regional artists working in various media from etching to oils. There are many images depicting Bosnian and Sarajevan scenes and landscapes. Prices range from 50 to 50.000KM.

Galerija Roman Petrović

Maršala Tita 54; tel. 033/688 009; genre: sculpture, photography and painting.

Umjetnička galerija BiH (National Gallery of Bosnia and Herzegovina)

Zelenih beretki 8; tel. 033/266 550; open: Tues-Sat 12-8pm; genre: a good selection of international and local artworks from the likes of Roy Lichenstein and Louise Bourgeois.

'To Be or Not To Be'

Čizmedžiluk 5

This is not even a commercial gallery but in fact a café which opened just before the war in 1992. It was a meeting place for artists to discuss art, exchange ideas, create and develop exhibitions. The original name was 'To Be or Not to Be' reflecting the artistic theme and philosophical nature of the venue. Once the war began the 'not to be' was crossed out as the 'to be' became symbolically important in expressing daily survival as the only focus for Sarajevo's citizens.

The café re-opened and now along the walls you can see original work by artists and evocative posters made during the war, all of which are for sale. It is possible to exhibit there and the owner is happy to view artists work for potential exhibitions. The café windows are also a kind of mini exhibition space displaying piles of ex-Yugoslavian paper money and a collection of antique objects and ceramic pots.

Art Market, Mediacentar

Kolodvorska 3 (about halfway down the street)

The first Sunday of the month sees art students and some local artists showing and selling their work, which is often really interesting and modestly priced. Open around 10-18 hours.

SICE (Sarajevo International Cultural Exchange) is a new art organisation whose mission statement is as follows:

"SICE is an annual international exchange project which allows artists to live and work together in Sarajevo irrespective of their country of origin and field of work. SICE has no obligation to political, ideological, economic interest or specific social mission. SICE will create a niche for itself in the arts and culture scene of Sarajevo and prepare the way for other projects."

I was lucky enough to attend the opening night of the 2004 exhibition and it was well worth visiting as much for the art and hobnobbing with the artists themselves as for the good party atmosphere.

The exhibition space is a disused factory on the right side of the lovely shady Vilsonovo šetalište just after you pass the back of the History Museum (to your right side). The artists in 2004 were from many different countries from the Netherlands to Japan and the work was diverse and challenging.

Contact:

Tel. 033 821 404

Email: siceinfo@web.de

Web: www.sarajevoice.com

Note: Artists wishing to exhibit at any venue mentioned here should contact the gallery concerned as all expressed they are happy to be approached. Selection is usually by portfolio presentation.

Green Sarajevo, *by Heather Day & Tim Clancy*

Sarajevo city is surrounded by greenery. You don't have to reach far from the urban buzz to find exquisite countryside. The region to which it belongs comprises stunning scenery of beautiful mountains, rivers, caves, gorges, waterfalls and ancient villages to explore. Bosnia and Herzegovina is 65% rural. Many locations, including all trails to the Skakavac waterfall near to Sarajevo, are perfectly safe to visit using clearly marked pathways. There's only really one mountain region which is no go without trained company and that is Treskavica Mountain. This leaves a myriad of mountains, hills and dales to explore. An opportunity not be missed. The usual sign for hiking paths is a painted red circle with a white centre.

The Parks of Sarajevo are not big by average European city standards but they are different and good places to have a cool moment during hot, sunny days.

Trg Oslobođenja is overlooked by the sunny coloured Orthodox Church. There is usually a group of old boys and the odd young'un playing chess with giant sized pieces. Everybody seems to get involved in telling the current player what to do and what not to do. You may witness a dramatic tantrum or heated exchange if the player fatally ignores advice wisely given. Its serious stuff you know!

There is a great chill out/relaxing stroll boulevard in Sarajevo called **Vilsonovo šetalište**. The trees here survived the desperate felling by freezing Sarajevans during the war as they were virtually on the front line. The area therefore was deserted during the war but is now open again as a shady haven for a peaceful walk along the river Miljacka.

At-Mejdan: This park is on the south side of the city and lies along the banks of the river. During the Ottoman Empire it was where horse exhibitions took place and the name means 'place of horses'. It was made in to a park in 1905, at the time of Austro-Hungarian rule, and renamed Franjo Josip after the Austrian king. During communism it carried the name of a Serbian Tzar. After the 1992-95 war the name again became At-Mejdan. Currently a replica of a Ottoman style bandstand is in construction. Apparently, it is a replica of an earlier building which stood there.

Veliki park: Meaning 'The Great Park', is located near the end of Maršala Tita at the junction with Koševo. The park was created in 1886 during Austrian Hungarian rule. It was built on the site of a Muslim cemetery and the old gravestones still cluster like mushrooms in the top end of the park. Bright white new graves from the more recent conflict are near the pavement side. It's funny that it's only as I am writing this that I realise the idea of a park/ graveyard where people sit chatting among tombstones may seem a bit morbid or at least unattractive. In fact for me being there does not feel spooky at all, poignant and thought provoking definitely but no less pleasant than any other public park. Sarajevo has a habit of subtly challenging your views or beliefs in general and offering something to satisfy the gap.

From the tram terminus Ilidža, you can cross the river to **Aleja (the alley)** a great tree-lined path 3 km long. You can take a horse and carriage along the path for 10 KM, but it's not too far to walk one way and horse it back. At the end of the Alley is Vrelo Bosne, the spring source of the river Bosna.

The natural park is laced by streams and little bridges. It's very picturesque and the breeze which drifts off the surface of the water is so refreshing it seems magical. The magic is possible because the temperature of the water is enough to freeze the balls off an Eskimo. On a sweltering summer's day your hot feet might cry out for a quick dip and it would be cruel to deny them but a full body emersion is only really possible for health freaks or Scandinavians.

There are also some tacky plastic boats for hire so you can glide in a 10 metre circle for a couple of KM. You can't really explore the streams this way because the bridges are so low it's impossible, but then it's just as well that the beauty of the waters isn't totally spoiled by hulking great pink swans. The boat depot is just beyond the main café area and works from 10-20 hours every day. The park has an area that is chocker with 'gifts' to buy and traditional fast food. Yes paradise and rough reality coexist however incongruously, but least you won't go hungry.

Please note: Stick to the main thoroughfares when walking along The Alley to Vrelo as mine clearance is ongoing in the surrounding fields. There are signs but it's as well to avoid wandering.

Tabia castle walls

The easiest way to find this place is to start from behind the National library and then walk to the hill on your left side. In summer the green areas around the fort on the hill overlooking the old town area of Sarajevo are full of local people chilling out, enjoying the lovely view and after dark the lights of the city.

Skakavac

Skakavac means grasshopper and the Skakavac waterfall is the largest constant flowing waterfall in Bosnia and Herzegovina. The stream that creates the 100m waterfall originates from four sources at the base of Bukovik Mountain to the north of Sarajevo. This is a popular picnic spot for locals. It has been placed under protection as a 'green belt' and has many hiking, biking and walking trails. The entire region is safe from mines and it is one of the closest places to Sarajevo for a nature excursion. Don't be intimidated by the burned-out mountain lodge that still sits in ruins near the falls. When the Dayton Peace Accords were signed, the Serbs abandoned many of the areas they had held and often set fire to what was left behind. This doesn't detract from the beautiful pine and beech tree forests, kilometres of great mountain biking or walking trails and the beautiful view of the waterfall. There are no facilities at the waterfall, though two places in the vicinity are almost ready to open their doors. The closest eatery currently open is the Lovački dom restaurant. This traditional restaurant serves fantastic local dishes. It is set in a lovely valley below eagle peaks, a little beyond the hunters' lodge. There is great terrain for walking, a pony ride for the kids and quite a few exotic animals running around. Try the young cheese (mladi sir) and beignets (uštipak) for starters. They also have a playground for children.

To get there by car

Head north out of town towards the Olympic Stadium on Patriotske lige Street. The road forks just before you reach the zoo. Staying to the right of the zoo the road turns into Nahorevska Street and continues to climb through the hills for about 3km. Although the road is curvy it is one road all the way to the falls. Once you reach the village of Nahorevo and the local shop or granap, you have three options: down to the right towards a small stream, back up to the left or straight along a single lane road. Go straight on and after about 1km the asphalt road will end. Continue climbing and stay on the main road. There will be an option to go down to the right, but just stay straight and after 9km you'll reach the waterfall area. It is only a ten-minute walk from the parking area to the falls, and there are signs and maps on location for the entire area.

To get there by bus

Go to the terminus of the number 69 bus to Nahovero which leaves from the top of Sutjeska Street near the American Embassy many times per day. I have listed the times here:

Week days
To Nahovero – 6.30, 7.15, 8.00, 9.00, 10.45, 11.35 and after about every hour

Saturday
To Nahorevo – every hour on the hour

Sunday and holidays
To Nahorevo – 6.55, 8.20, 9.45, 11.05, 12.35 and after every few hours

Although this information is correct at the time of writing, it may change and it's always best to check times, especially for the return journey. The journey is no more than about 30 minutes.

From the village you have a 2-3 hour marked walk through glorious nature to the falls.

Barice and Čavljak

High above the city to the northeast is a plateau named Barice. The municipality of Stari Grad (old town) has begun developing this part of the 'city' as a recreation area. There is a large parking and picnic facility with several café's and restaurants in Barice. The main road leading to Barice may not be the easiest one to find but there is a main asphalt road that leads all the way to the top. The forest on both sides of the last section of the road before you reach the mine-free plateau is heavily mined. It is clearly marked and you are advised to just keep driving to the parking area. Once you reach the Barice parking the trails and roads are totally mine free.

Čavljak is another few kilometres up the road – there is an asphalt road leading to a brand new mountain lodge. One can hike up or drive. The hiking area near Čavljak is vast and totally free of mines. Čavljak Mountian Lodge is owned and operated by the Džemal Bijedić Mountain Association. It is a restaurant-café with stunning views of the city (the lodge is at 1,250 meters). They also have a sleeping capacity of around 25 – dormitory style. A half board costs around 20 KM or 10 euros. The place is simple but clean, new and comfortable. They have guides that can take you hiking as well for a minimal fee. Being only 9 kilometers from town it is a great place to spend the day, even with children. If you are backpacking and just want to a few days in the city and more time in nature – you can't beat this deal!

Guided exploring and hiking

There's really no need to fret unnecessarily about the presence of land mines in Bosnia as any public areas have been well and carefully cleared. Bosnia is a gorgeous land full of fantastic natural beauty and I would not wish to discourage enjoyment of this, however when visiting the countryside and mountains it is wise to keep to officially safe routes or to travel with an experienced guide.

Green Visions is a pioneer organisation promoting excellent, eco-aware activities to suit adventurous souls. All tour leaders are experienced guides.

Outing options: Day walks and hikes, tour and cross country skiing, highland village tourism, rafting, cultural excursions, mountain hut rental, mountain bikes, climbing, flora and fauna expeditions.

Contact details: Office – Radnička bb, 71000 Sarajevo, tel: 033 717 290, mobile: 061 213 278, e-mail: sarajevo@greenvisions.ba, web: www.greenvisions.ba

Fikret Kahrović is an individual who leads walks generally on Sundays (and speaks good English).

Usually you need to find your own way to the starting points and bring a packed lunch. Sometimes longer trips of a few days are arranged and naturally in this case additional accommodation fees apply. Tel: 061 379 915, e-mail: fikret6@hotmail.com

The Mountaineering Society

They have walks and hikes for members but it's possible to participate. You will need to reach starting points on your own steam and take your own food etc. At the office you can pick up information about mountain huts to stay in which punctuate hiking routes through the Bjelašnica mountain. Office: Zelenih beretki 15, tel: 033 535 371, e-mail: pdbjelasnica@yahoo.com

If you are hiking you may come across small houses where the inhabitants prepare food. At Crepoljsko in the Bukovik mountain region, near to Skakavac waterfall, there is such a place. The food available generally is:

Čorba - Meat and vegetable soup

Uštipak - Hot dough sausages in which you put white cheese

Proja - Savory cake with spinach

Šampinjoni - Mushrooms (local and wild) cooked in delicious sauce

*The wonderful green mountain lining most of the southside of the Miljacka Valley in Sarajevo is called Trebević Mountain. It's gorgeous pine trees and superb location for scenic viewpoints tend to draw interested travellers to it. Unfortunately my friends, we recommend you stay away unless you're with a local guide. Trebević saw some ugly fighting during the war and is riddled with landmines. Just to be on the safe – don't go on Trebević.

ILIDŽA

Situated 12km southwest of Sarajevo, Ilidža has long been a close retreat for city dwellers to enjoy the thermal springs, recreation centre and the lovely park at the source of River Bosna called **Vrelo Bosna**. The park has acres of lush green fields, gushing fresh waters that spring from the surrounding mountains, a recently upgraded park where children can play and two tasty traditional restaurants near one of the largest cascades in the park. I definitely recommend weekday visits during the summer; weekends are crowded and this tends to take away the tranquil ambience of the park. The springs are accessible by car, foot, bike or horse and carriage. The long tree-lined **aleja** is closed to vehicle traffic and is perfect for a jog, walk or bike ride. It is possible to take a 10KM horse and carriage ride from the top of the avenue in an old carriage from the Austro-Hungarian period. This is the only place in Bosnia and Herzegovina that still practises this tradition. The Austrian nobility were particularly fond of this area and many luxurious houses from that period were built in the area around the sources. Not far from the source is the Roman bridge. Although it resembles a Roman bridge it is of Ottoman design. The bridge was merely named after the ancient settlers of this region.

If you are looking for less expensive accommodation than found in the centre of town, Ilidža has many good hotels and can be up to 20% cheaper. Ilidža is connected to Sarajevo by regular buses and the trams travel all day to the city centre and back.

Hotel Casa Grande (Velika aleja 2; tel: 033 637 655; email: casagrande@casagrande-bih.com; web: www.casagrande-bih.com) is one of the best hotels in Ilidža but is priced the same as its downtown competition. The Viennese-style building is one of the many large villas built along the aleja during Austrian rule in Bosnia in the early 1900s. Single rooms are around 90KM, doubles are 140KM and they have great, fully equipped apartments for 180KM. Some of the rooms are slightly odd. A chandelier that is not connected to electricity, a seating area in a room without windows, mirrors that force you to look at yourself sitting on the toilet – that sort of thing.

Hotel Hollywood (Dr Mustafe Pintola 23; tel: 033 773 100; email: hollywood@bih.net.ba; web: www.hotel-hollywood.com.ba) is a nice, reasonably priced spot in the centre of Ilidža. Singles go for 75KM and doubles run from 120KM. It's a great bargain for tourist-class couples.

Hotel Delminium (Bare 16H; tel: 033 627 667; fax: 033 636 598; email: info@delminium.co.ba; web: www.delminium.co.ba) is owned by the same folk who run the classy Restaurant Dubrovnik in downtown Sarajevo. With about 40 beds they offer single rooms for 75KM and doubles for 120KM.

Oaza (Četvrte viteške brigade 3, Ilidža; tel: 033 636 142/141; fax: 033 636 140) is 15km from town. Besides the hotel there are small bungalows that are the same price as single and double rooms at 55KM and 70KM respectively. It is the only place in town where you can park your camper. It even has suitable plug-ins and facilities.

Hotel Terme Hrasnička cesta 14, 033 772 000/2, has been a thermal healing spa since Roman times. The Austrian-Hungarian empire capitalized on the healing waters and built a hotel complex and thermal center. Hotel Terme has been recently renovated and is now probably the best spa in the entire country. The facilities are brand new and they offer a wide range of therapies; including hydro, physical, and recreational. There are two pools and a state of the art physical fitness center that are accessible to all guests.

The food and service are excellent. The restaurant is also new and offers a wide range of good quality meals. Staff are friendly and helpful. The hotel also offers great ski packages – you can ski on the Olympic Mountains (transport provided by the hotel), and come back to a Jacuzzi or sauna before heading downtown for a night out. The rooms are newly renovated and are spacious and comfortable. Singles are 60/80KM and doubles are 80/120KM.

The **Ciklo Centar** (Hamze Ćelenke 58, Sarajevo 71000; tel: 033 625 243; email: bikeshop@bih.net.ba; web: www.ciklocentar.com) rents out mountain bikes and can arrange excursions. Nino, the owner, and his mountain biking team organize 1-3 day biking trips in the highlands of Bjelašnica and Visočica. They are very experienced, have good equipment, provide professional service and always have a trail vehicle on for the long hauls. Anyone interested in a fun and challenging mountain bike trip should go with them, as these people know the mountain trails better than anybody else.

SHOPPING

Sarajevo has an ancient tradition of handicrafts in leather, metal, wood, textiles, shoes, gold, carpets and rugs ... and just about any practical thing you can think of. Many of these trades were brought here from Persia and Turkey during the Ottoman period, as well as from Dubrovnik, or ancient Ragusa. It wasn't too long ago that Sarajevans made almost everything they needed in life, from the basic necessities to luxury items for the more fortunate. This tradition has been passed down for many generations, from father to son and from mother to daughter.

The more modern styles in clothes and shoes are mainly from western Europe. However, you may find some high-quality Italian shoes much cheaper than you'd find at home. The true value of shopping in Sarajevo though is in finding the old crafts ... called stari zanati in Bosnian.

Stari zanati developed with the arrival of the Ottomans in the mid 15th century. As the city expanded into the administrative centre of Ottoman rule in Bosnia so did its volume of trade with far away lands. Many crafts were brought by the Ottomans to keep the soldiers in good footwear, make swords and design and create more modern weaponry for the military. By the early 15th century the Ottoman defters (administrative records) registered more than 19 new crafts including coppersmiths, locksmiths, slipper makers and carpenters.

Craftsmanship continued to develop during the first half of the 100-year occupation. Tailoring, clock-making, and quilt-making were famous trades by the end of the 17th century. By the end of Ottoman rule over 70 zanati trades are mentioned in historical records, as Sarajevo developed into the largest trading town in all of Bosnia and Herzegovina.

As the trade centre in the old town developed certain streets became 'blacksmith' streets and others 'goldsmith' streets. In time each craft was located in a particular part of town as is seen today. Today you'll find Kazazi Street named after the silk tailors, Kazandžiluk named after the coppersmiths and Mudželeti named after the bookbinders. Each craft was headed by a mastercraftsman or ćehaja and they formed official bodies, representing their craft to the local government.

Baščaršija is filled with shops of stari zanati. Prices for handmade goods are very reasonable and local vendors are usually willing to bargain with you. When compared to prices at home for handmade goods, the craft shops in Sarajevo are a bargain. Take advantage of it! Bezistan, on the main walkway Ferhadija, is a lovely market with many shops and the entire area around Sebilj is lined with shops. Check out the stari zanati website at www.starizanati.co.ba.

If you're looking for oriental spices and some amazing sweets and nuts then pay a visit to Butik Badem on Abadžiluk 12. The Turkish delights and candied almonds are something you've got to try. I promise you'll find something you fancy there. For those of you on a mission to find oriental or Bosnian rugs and carpets there are many shops in the old town that specialise in 'ćilim's.' Bulbul at Abadžiluk 13a are very knowledgeable and have a variety of old and new rugs from Bosnia and around the Balkans. Isfahan Persian Rugs at Sarači 57 and 77, one located inside Morića han, is run by an art historian. He's an enthusiastic gentleman with loads of information on the origins of persian art and rugs. Kiko at Trgovke 19 in Baščaršija has a nice selection of new and used rugs. They are local specialists and also have a repair service.

Gift and souvenir shops are in abundance in the old town. Some of the best handmade gift shops are run by women's clubs or refugee consortiums. If you are exploring the old town, try to find NUR. It is hidden in a little side street of the silver- and gold jewellery street, the address is Veliki ćurčiluk 35. They sell bags, hats, dresses, skirts and coats that are handmade and painted by the owner. They have a bit of an old fashioned look, but that is part of their charm.

If you are lucky, you can see the artists at work because they paint the clothes and accessories during opening hours.

Another must see in the old town is 'Kao pao shu'. This shop is owned by three fashion designers who took part in Sarajevo Fashion Week and who design upon request. Unfortunately, we were not able to go there for an interview or to have some clothes made, because the girls were on holiday. But from what I have heard their designs are smashing and they really pay attention to you and what would suit you. So if you are looking for something special, it is definitely worth having a look.

The Bosnian Handicraft Knitwear Shop at Čizmedžiluk 1 sells handmade sweaters, gloves, scarves and toys made by Bosnian women. Logo Asian Trading Company on Skenderija is run by a member of the International Women's Club which deals in lamps, mirrors, dishes and jewellery. Melanie Gift Shop at Sime Milutinovića 15 has beautiful pictures, souvenirs and handmade cards. There are dozens more. An unemployed art teacher named Vahida Ključa creates lovely pictures of old town settings made out of corn stalk and dried flowers. She doesn't have a shop but you can email her at vahida@yahoo.com or call 033 457 526 to view her work. I came across her art at a Christmas bazaar run by the women's club and bought presents for my whole family from her.

A bit of change

Tattoo and piercing studios, *By Heather Day*

Permanently decorating the body doesn't seem to be massively popular in Sarajevo. Of three licensed tattoo parlours only one remains open for business. It is **Tattoo Paja** Shopping precinct Skenderija; tel: 061 158 987 / 061 105 8946; open Monday - Saturday from 9am – 6pm.

This is a small business and currently the only professional one in central Sarajevo. It is not exactly plush and the huge 'mural' of the grim reaper holding back a rabid dog might make you think twice about being there. However, I did have a peek behind the customer modesty curtain and it appeared that the premises are clean and tidy. There are plenty of images showing previous clients freshly tattooed and folders full of images and original art works if you need help choosing a design.

If there's a queue you can also find a pretty good range of dated tattoo magazines to leaf through.

In addition to tatoos, the range of services they offer includes permanent make-up, cover-up, re-working and/or fixing or old tattoos and piercing of all types in all areas of the body.

Other things you may want to buy

- Also in Ferhadija, there is Edo. This man runs a shoe shop under the same name. He measures your feet and makes shoes accordingly within a week (or two, sometimes). Edo uses first-class material and his shoes are great. Hovering around 200 KM, they cost a lot less than what hand-made shoes cost in the West.
- There are many books about Sarajevo and the country. Some are about the war, but there are some more relaxing coffee table books as well, with themes such as maps, paintings, poems, pictures, jewels and bridges. You will find the best collections at **buybook** (Radićeva 4 and Zelenih beretki 8), Sejtarija (Maršala Tita 19) and Šahinpašić (Mula-Mustafe Bašeskije 1). They all have English language novels and newspapers as well. For online book purchases: www.interliber.com.
- There are a lot of very specialist shops, shops that sell nothing but coffee, organic herbal teas or all sorts of honey, or oriental sweets. Close to the SFOR Butmir base, you will find an (ever decreasing as SFOR is scaling down) number of shops that sell nothing but English-language CD's and DVD's for rock-bottom prices. In the old town, there are a few people in the open markets that sell all sorts of local music.

Fashion in Sarajevo,
by Babeth Knol and Vincent Braconnay

Sitting on the sidewalk in front of Rotterdam central station, I was waiting for the bus that would take me to Sarajevo. I had just rolled out of bed and yawned for the sixtieth time since I did. There was a little piece of bread in my hair from the early breakfast, but fortunately someone pointed that out to me before I got on the bus. Probably because I was not feeling very fashionable myself I noticed something strange about the three other girls getting on the bus. In spite of the early hour, they were all dressed impeccable. Their faces looked pretty with carefully applied make-up, and they even wore very elegant shoes. They maintained that appearance during the entire 30 hour bus trip. I was very impressed.

And when I arrived in Sarajevo, feeling a bit shabby myself, I could see more of these well groomed young people (both women and men) all around the city. People that are into fashion or watching beautiful people should have a great time in Sarajevo. There are many terraces where you can sit down to spot the latest trends and the smashing looking people wearing them, and of course there are many shops where you can buy all those fashionable items.

If you feel like exploring Sarajevo's shopping possibilities, check the fashion and shop reviews below.

Trendspotting
It is always good to visit a terrace when you are travelling. A somewhat comfortable chair, a drink, some friends or just by yourself, enjoying the sun if you are lucky. If you like to watch people, add one good element to your terrace experience in Sarajevo.

There are trendy places all around, but there are some that are especially good for seeing and meeting fashionable people.

In the centre, those bars are 'City Pub' and 'Central Café'. If you want to find some people that are fashionable in a more alternative way, go to the boulevard in front of the school for fine arts (the big yellow building on the other side of the bridge) where a lot of people hang out every night, or go there and enter so.ba for a drink.

For my trendspotting experience, I went to Central Café with a friend. It was wonderful. You could literally see the latest trends walk by just enjoying your drink. We spent hours there.

The trend for this summer (2004) was as follows:

For men: The shirts are tight, same can go for the trousers. Shabby looks are not fashionable here, guys in Sarajevo seem to take a massive effort to show off their body, to coordinate the colours they wear and to have a matching hairstyle. T-shirts have brand names or texts such as 'fuck war' and 'let life be progressive'. 'Advertising' t-shirts are trendy as well, I saw a Fanta one and many from organisations around town. The most popular hairdo is short and messy (styled messy) in front, and long at the back. The accessory is of course a pair of big celebrity looking sunglasses.

For women, it seems to be that less is more. They can get away with very little tops and skirts in Sarajevo, which makes the streets look like a music video at some times. While the amount of fabric is very small, the amount of colours is enormous. Especially bright colours such as yellow, pink, lime green and baby blue are very hot. You can see a lot of printed t-shirts with texts like 'I'm too cool to be a fool', 'Barbie is dead', 'how do you spell fool b-o-y-s' and 'I'm looking for a rich guy'

The hair is usually long and shiny, some girls adapted the boys' trendy haircut and have the front short and ponytail(s) at the back. Accessories are handbags in matching colour with clothes, big sunglasses, high heels and if wanted, it is possible to wear lots and lots of make-up.

Final remark on the trendspotting: After spending some hours on the terrace, having a couple of drinks, maybe a cake (you should, they are very good), you might feel a bit guilty dietwise. Almost every person walking by has the figure of a supermodel. But don't worry about that. I heard that going to the gym is not as popular here as you would assume. People probably just spend a lot of time and lose a lot of cakes walking up and down the city streets every day. Just join them in their pleasant exercise.

Market (pijaca)

When we were asking people about their favourite shops in Sarajevo, the more alternative looking people pointed us to the market. According to them, it was just not possible to find any alternative clothes in the city. What most of them do is buying cheap clothes on the market and personalizing them. Either by cutting and sewing them together and adjust the form, by painting something on it or just by wearing some special jewellery on it.

There is one very central market, just at the beginning of Ferhadija, close to the eternal flame. In my opinion, you would have to look very hard to find nice clothes on that market, but the prices are very low and it might be worth the effort. And if you do not find any clothes, have a look at the cd and dvd stands. They are illegal copies, but there are many good local movies and cd's on sale that would be difficult to find in music stores in other countries.

Skenderija

If it is raining, or if you would like to see what's on the other side of the river, there is an inside shopping centre called Skenderija just after the school of fine arts (if you are coming from the side of the old town). Admittedly, I did not really like it when I first entered. It looks a bit dirty because of the brown colour and the shop windows that are overly crowded because they show almost every item in the store. But if you look beyond that, it is possible to find some nice things here. There are a lot of shops that sell sneakers and sportswear and a lot of shops with the same trendy and colourful clothes you see in the centre, but also a store with very nice bags, a bookstore and a shop called Monte that sells beautiful ballroom dresses from Istanbul.

You can find some café's and a casino called Coloseum Club in Skenderija as well.

Unitic

If you feel like shopping in a luxurious environment, you should go to Unitic. If you are coming from the city centre, you can just walk by the main road Maršala Tita, and when you come to Marijin Dvor, you will see its two glass towers from there. The address is Fra Anđela Zvizdovića 1. The building is very modern and seems to be built up entirely from glass, which beautifully reflects the old houses and the church across the street. If you go up the stairs and enter the building, you will see a lot of clean and modern interior design as well. The towers house offices of banks, insurance companies and big international aid organisations, and on ground level there are some congress rooms. The stores (that are on ground level and downstairs) sell things that are mostly interesting for business people, like suitcases, computers and flights. But the stock seems to be growing. A quite expensive but fabulous shoe shop opened on the first floor, there is a trendy hairdresser downstairs and there are some fashion shops which stand out because of the effort they put into the shop windows and interior design.

Although most of the articles sold in Unitic are for the rich shopper, you can find some very affordable (20 KM/10 Euro) clothes as well.

SKIING

For many of you, Sarajevo will not only remind you of its grim recent past – but of its glorious debut as Winter Olympic Game hosts in 1984. Twenty four hours away from the opening ceremonies, Sarajevo and the surrounding mountains had little or no snow. It was a disaster waiting to happen – or was it? The Sarajevo Miracle occurred on the eve of the XIV Winter Olympics – it snowed and snowed and snowed. I remember watching it as a kid on the TV, but ask a Sarajevan old enough to remember and eyes will light up and stories of the first and only Olympics ever held in the former Yugoslavia will come pouring out.

The glory days have passed for now, but the Olympic style skiing most certainly has not. The considerable war damage to the Bjelašnica and Igman Mountain ski centers has largely been repaired, and Jahorina never saw much war damage to begin with. Both offer great skiing and snowboarding for a mere fraction of the prices charged in ski resorts in the west. There aren't any high-tech modern lifts and posh alpine villas, but no one can dispute the quality of the slopes, snow and fun to be had skiing on these Olympic mountains.

JAHORINA MOUNTAIN

Jahorina is the mountain range to the southeast of Sarajevo. Its ideal geographical position more or less guarantees three to four months of good ski snow. Its highest peak reaches 1,910m. The ski lifts climb to 1,894m with fabulous views towards Sarajevo. The slopes of Jahorina are covered in tall pines till about the 1,500m mark. From there the mountainside is relatively bare with some thick patches of klek, a high-altitude pine that doesn't grow higher than 2m.

Getting there

Jahorina is easily accessible via two routes. The Sarajevo-Pale road is a 20 minute drive and from Pale the ride to the top takes another 20 minutes. Alternatively, from the airport you travel southeast before taking a left towards Lukavica. This road climbs, winds and meanders all the way to Jahorina via Trebević Mountain, overlooking the city of Sarajevo. It is one road all the way up and very straightforward once you start the climb. The Trebević road is considerably longer than the Pale route. During the winter months it could take an hour to reach Jahorina. However, it is by far the most attractive road, with stunning views of the city.

Where to stay and eat

Hotel Crystal Tel: 057 226 574/226 725. Built in 2001 in an Alpine mountain style, this is a nice and new hotel. The rooms are excellent with good food to match. Rooms have satellite TV, minibar and bath. The hotel also has a bar, restaurant, sauna and ski rental (and service). It is the only place on Jahorina where guests have garage facilities, which are great for the really cold days. It is wise to make reservations a few months ahead of time.

Hotel Košuta Tel: 057 270 401. The atmosphere of the hotel is warm and cosy with nice, simple rooms and a great menu of traditional foods. They often organize live traditional music. They also have local pop, which is an acquired taste. Košuta offers a full range of services and is located near the top where the main slopes are. There is a disco which is also more to the local liking. The food, service and location are certainly amongst the best on Jahorina. Advanced reservations are recommended from December to late January.

Hotel Bistrica Tel: 057 270 020. This is the largest hotel that was built specifically for the Olympics. It is located 1,620m (5,000 feet) above sea level. Bistrica's interior still embraces the socialist style, particularly in the rooms. They are comfortable enough but nowhere near Western standard. The restaurant and bar serve good traditional food and it offers by far the best view on the mountain. It is the only hotel on Jahorina with an indoor swimming pool and weight room. The hotel also owns a small pension called Poljice named after the valley in which it is located. It too is very near the ski lifts and is a smaller alternative to the large, state-run Hotel Bistrica.

Pansion Sport Tel: 057 270 444. Located in the Poljice Valley on Jahorina, the Pansion Sport prides itself on the national dishes it serves in its restaurant Kamin (meaning fireplace). It is a medium-sized pension with basic rooms. There is a ski and snowboard rental and thay have professional instructors. The ski lifts are nearby.

Vila Golden Wheat Tel: 057 270 038 / 025, 065 950 842 is a tiny new villa with five rooms and two apartments. The rooms are basic but nice with wood interiors. Only the apartments have satellite TV. The restaurant is more like a fast-food grill and in the basement is a café-bar with a fireplace. They offer ski rental and servicing.

There are several restaurants not tied to the hotels and they are right at the bottom of the ski trails. The food is by and large traditional and finding a seat is the greatest challenge of the day.

What to see and do

This north face mountain was home to many of the competitions of the 1984 Winter Olympic Games. The resorts and infrastructure escaped the ravages of war and several new hotels have been erected in the past few years. Jahorina is the largest ski area in the country. It has 12 lifts all over the mountain that offer Olympic-style professional trails and novice trails for children and beginners. The high season on Jahorina is mid-December to late January. Around the new year it is almost impossible to get accommodation without advance reservations. An alternative for last-minute travellers is to book a hotel in Sarajevo, then drive to Jahorina as it is only about 45 minutes from town. On the mountain you will find the full range of facilities including an indoor swimming pool, medical centre, information centres, ski rentals, restaurants and café's, skiing instruction in English and internet access.

One advantage to skiing in Bosnia, whether on Jahorina, Bjelašnica or Vlašić, is the incredibly low cost of just about anything. Don't expect, however, to find five-star resorts or high-tech lifts. The basics are provided and the skiing is, well, good enough for the Olympics!

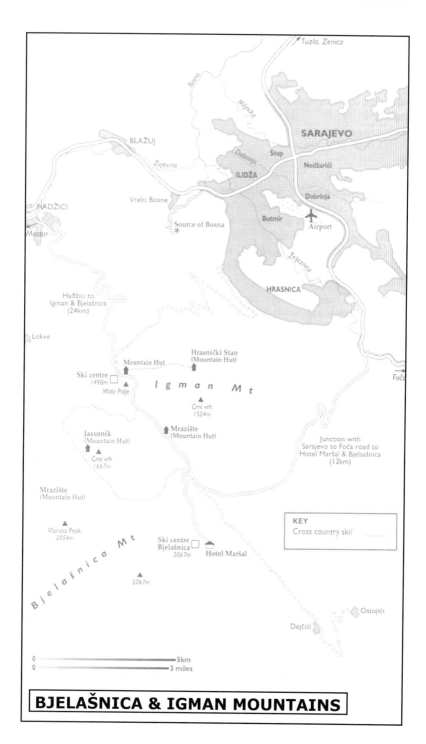

BJELAŠNICA & IGMAN MOUNTAINS

BJELAŠNICA AND IGMAN MOUNTAINS

These two names are synonymous with the 1984 Winter Olympic Games. Most of the infrastructure in this region was destroyed during the war, as were many of the traditional highland villages. A single-track dirt road over Igman constituted the only access route into Sarajevo during the war while Bjelašnica was the buffer zone between the Bosnian government army and Bosnian Serb militaries. French United Nations 'peacekeepers' were stationed at the ski centre for a good part of the conflict.

The Dayton Accords gave this part of the mountain to the Federation, linking it with the city from which it had been cut off for so many years. Some reconstruction has been completed and plans for building a large youth hostel have been approved. It is anticipated that there will be significant reconstruction of and investment into this area in the near future, and there is a very strong lobby to proclaim Bjelašnica/Igman a national park.

There are currently three lifts operational on these mountains. Bjelašnica has the best infrastructure and most challenging slopes while Igman is a bit easier and also has a children's lift with soft hills to practice on. Bjelašnica has the steepest of all slopes – racing from almost 2,000 meters to the base at 1,200 meters. It's quite a rush – no lines, no waiting.

Getting there

From Sarajevo via East Sarajevo (or "Srpsko Sarajevo", as it was called until recently), there are signs marked for Hotel Maršal about 6km east of the airport. There is only one right turn to be made at the large quarry and that road leads directly to the ski centre and the hotel. From the centre of town the drive takes approximately 45 minutes. There are no Sarajevo-based buses that travel on this route. From the suburb of Ilidža though there are minibuses that travel twice daily to Igman-Bjelašnica-Sinanovići via Hadžići. The cost is a mere 2KM. From the south the best access route is again from Hadžići (20km south of Sarajevo centre). In the middle of Hadžići is a single road that leads directly to Igman. There is only one road so it is nearly impossible to get lost once you're on the right route. The distance from Hadžići to Bjelašnica is 24km.

Where to stay

Hotel Maršal Tel: 033 279 100; fax: 033 279 149; email: marshal@pksa.com.ba; web: www.hotel-marsal.ba. Currently the only hotel on the mountain, Maršal sticks out like a sour thumb. It is located at the base of the ski lifts, has space for about 70 guests and is a bargain for those accustomed to the outrageous prices at ski resorts in the West. During the ski season prices are 70-100KM for a single room and 125-180KM for a double depending on the month. In the off-season the cost for a single/double room is only 55/80KM. All the rooms have satellite TV and phone and the decor is brand new. They have a restaurant and bar that serves international and traditional foods. There is also a fast food bar, a disco and a billiards room. The best fun is outside though. The ski lifts are three minutes away. Ski rentals and lessons for beginners (in English) are available in the hotel.

Construction of other accommodation has begun and the provision of bed and breakfast in the surrounding villages is in the stage of development.

Where to eat

The plateau at the base of the ski runs has several restaurants. Restaurant **Planinska kuća** serves authentic highland dishes and has a great traditional atmosphere. Even in the high season the prices are very reasonable, a meal with a drink costing 12-14KM. The homemade pita (spinach or cheese pie) is the house specialty and is absolutely delicious. The **Benetton Restaurant** run by the ski centre is open only during the season and serves fast food and drinks in a large, hangar-like building. **Aroma** is just next to Maršal and serves only traditional food. The food is very good quality with very low prices. Don't expect many veggies as meat and stew is the order of the day in most mountain places.

On Igman Mountain there is a traditional restaurant, **Mražište,** at the ski centre which often has light live music. The menu is a typical traditional one and most of the food is from the surrounding mountain villages. The food is excellent, especially after a few runs.

What to see and do

The skiing area on Bjelašnica has been rebuilt. Bjelašnica is the steepest of Bosnia's ski mountains. From the peak at 2,067m (over 6,250ft) the steep slopes quickly bring you to the bottom at 1,200m (3,600ft). Lift tickets are extremely cheap. One-day passes cost 18KM and provided there are no ridiculous queues you can easily get in a dozen runs in a day. There are medical and toilet facilities on site as well as a mountain rescue team.

A few miles from the slopes of Bjelašnica are the ski runs on Igman Mountain, the north face of Bjelašnica. Igman hosted the ski-jumping competition during the Olympics and has several good but smaller routes. There is also a children's area and a small lift for beginners. Igman is ideal for families and even has horse-drawn carriage rides through the snow. There are ski rentals here as well (for as little as 12KM per day) and the ski-lift passes are the same price as on Bjelašnica.

In the valley of Ravna Vala is a long cross-country route that was also used during the Olympics. Although the trails are not in pre-war condition, they are more than suitable for terrific cross-country skiing, hiking and walking.

AROUND SARAJEVO

The very title 'Around Sarajevo' may be open to interpretation. In this instance it refers to the territories east of Sarajevo, to a few areas to the immediate north and to the Bjelašnica and Igman Mountains to the south. Other areas are covered in the other booklets in this series.

HIGHLAND VILLAGES

The highland villages of Bjelašnica and neighbouring Visočica Mountain have long been famous for their folklore, organic food, and traditional architec-

The largest medieval cemetery in the Sarajevo region on Mt. Bjelašnica

There is more than skiing on Jahorina, Bjelašnica and Igman

Jahorina's Mountain is the country's finest Olympic Ski resort.

Plenty of fun for ski and snow board lovers!

Sarajevo hosts some of the finest and most inexpensive Olympic
quality skiing in southern Europe

ture and lifestyles. Many of these villages were destroyed during the war but have been rebuilt, albeit not in their traditional form. The villages give a last peek into old-world Europe and the traditional ways of life that have long since died out in the West.

Lukomir

At almost 1,500m, the village of Lukomir, with its unique stone homes with cherry-wood roof tiles, is the highest and most isolated village in the country. Indeed, access to the village is impossible from the first snows in December until late April and sometimes even later, except by skis or on foot. A newly constructed lodge is now complete, and will hopefully soon open the village to receive guests in a mountain house that is rather luxurious compared to how the local people live. From there, you can do some magnificent hiking in the area along the ridge of the **Rakitnica Canyon**, which drops 800m below.

Lukomir is known for its traditional attire, and the women still wear the hand-knitted costumes that have been worn for centuries. It is said that local shepherds from the Konjic area fled here during the middle ages in protest of the rule of the Bosnian Kingdom and even perhaps the Catholic church. These heretics sought refuge in this extremely isolated place and called it 'Luka mira', 'Oasis of Peace'. With the arrival of Islam, they converted the name of the village to Lukomir. In another version of history, the present-day residents of Lukomir can trace much of their ancestory to the Podveležje region of Herzegovina. These semi-nomadic tribes would come to Bjelašnica in the summer months because of the abundance of water. Podveležje, a dry plateau above Mostar, could not provide the herds with enough water to sustain themselves over the summer months. The trek to Lukomir would take three days across some of the most difficult mountain terrain in the country. For reasons not entirely known, many of the villagers from the Podveležje region eventually made permanent settlements in the canyon and later in the place where it is now located.

The local villagers are shepherds who live off the sale of sheep and milk products and almost completely rely on what mother nature provides. The handmade socks you might find for sale in the village are not just a little hand-made. The wool is manually cut with scizzors and cooked and cleaned by hand. The socks are meant to be warm and waterproof, and producing them takes a considerable amount of time. Please keep that in mind when you are trying to bargain with them – the material wasn't bought ready-made in a shop, but made with the hardworking hands you'll see on every man, woman and child in this village.

Umoljani

Umoljani village is more easily accessible than Lukomir. The village was destroyed during the war, but by now much of it has been rebuilt. The natural beauty of its surroundings is the most striking in the area. The south side is a typical karst landscape that is dry and rather barren. The north side is lush with thick forest and green pastures and is ideal for hiking, walking or a picnic. The remnants of ancient settlers can be found scattered around the village with many medieval tombstones perched on high ridges. The valley of Studeno Polje is a magical little place tucked behind the summer shepherd village of Gradina near Umoljani.

The Legend of Umoljani Village

During Ottoman times a small village in the Bjelašnica highlands had to face its own demons. There were rumours of a dragon-like creature roaming in the foothills of Obalj Mountain. Some shepherds swore they saw it, others claimed to have lost sheep to the creature. The villagers were panic stricken. The local Muslim priest (Hodža) decided to go and find this dragon. He expected to find nothing but asked the villagers to pray for him while he was gone. For days there was no sign of the hodža and the scared villagers diligently prayed. Then, as rumour has it, the hodža met the beast just above the shepherds' summer huts. He too used prayer as his main weapon and in an instant the dragon was frozen in stone on top of the mountain. The hodža returned with the news. He gave credit to the faith and prayers of the villagers for his impossible victory and named the village Umoljani, meaning 'of the prayers.' On a peak just above the village of Umoljani is a rock formation that very much resembles a dragon's tail.

During the last war the entire village was destroyed with the exception of the mosque. The story goes that before the war a Serbian commander's son was sick and none of the doctors could heal or even diagnose him. He heard of a powerful hodža in the village of Umoljani and took his son there. The hodža miraculously healed the ailing boy in the mosque. Several years later, when the Serbian military burned down the village, the commander was the father of the healed boy. Out of superstition, guilt or who knows what, he spared the mosque, which is now the only remaining mosque of its type on Bjelašnica Mountain.

Šabići village is located only 15 minutes from Maršal Hotel and the Bjelašnica ski slopes. Here, the local community has attempted to preserve the stećci and have created a necropolis in the centre of the village. The village is 1,160m above sea level and rests in the upper valley of the Rakitnica River. Šabići acts as a centre for the other highland villages and is the only village with a school and medical clinic. There is also a hunting lodge.

Rakitnica, another village close to the Bjelašnica ski slopes, used to be the most beautiful representative of the Bjelašnica highland settlements. Its houses were made of wood and many of the homes were over 150 years old. Unfortunately the village was totally destroyed by Serbian forces during the war. The reconstruction of the village is complete but with modern design.

Bobovica sits high on the ridge above Rakitnica Canyon, on the north slopes of Visočica Mountain. The village has stunning panoramic views of Bjelašnica, Visočica and Treskavica mountains. There are well-maintained trails that travel deep into the steep canyon as well as to the high, sharp peaks of Visočica. **Sinanovići** is in the near vicinity of Bobovica and has several places to eat and stay overnight in traditional bed and breakfasts. It is situated in the valley of Tušilačka River which is a tributary of Rakitnica River. The area around the village is famous for its beautiful meadows, covered by wild flowers in the spring. Much of the village has been restored in traditional style. There is a mountain lodge run by the **Treskavica Moun-**

tain Association (tel: 033 239 031) that offers meals and accommodation. It is best to travel with a guide in this region as trails are not well marked and there are mined areas within three miles of the village. There is a public bus line that travels along the main mountain routes from Ilidža via Maršal-Šabići-Umoljani to the vicinity of Bobovica and Sinanovići.

Ostojići and Dejčići villages are located further down the main road from Sarajevo, towards the Bjelašnica Ski Centre. There are well-marked signs and a paved road that leads to both villages. These villages are set on the northeast side of Bjelašnica Mountain and host the largest medieval graveyards in Sarajevo canton. These relics from Bosnia's heretic Christians mark the significance of highland life, dating back to the earliest Slavic settlers who assimilated with the indigenous Illyrian tribes as far back as the 7th century. There is a youth centre in Dejčići and accommodation is available in the homes of the villagers. This area too has mines on the upper slopes a few miles from the village and, although access to the village is perfectly safe, it is recommended to travel with a guide only.

Rakitnica Canyon

I have quite a dilemma in writing this – let me tell you why. If you love nature, there will be a few times in your life when you find a place that strikes you as so sacred you want to either keep it to yourself or simply accept the fact that there are places on this earth that humans do not need to go. This is that place – a rugged and painfully beautiful canyon that stretches twenty five kilometers between Bjelašnica and Visočica Mountains to southeast of Sarajevo.

The ancient pine and beech tree forests hide all the fairies from us. Bears, wolves, wild boar, pine martens and wild goats all take refuge in this difficult-to-access canyon. The canyon stretches 26km and feeds the Neretva River in Herzegovina near Konjic. Rakitnica is a natural wonderland. Hundreds of thousands of years of tectonic shifts have created the steep limestone walls of Visočica and Bjelašnica mountains. The crystal-clear river below is created by the melting snow and the hundreds of underground aquifer systems, making Rakitnica River water potable for the entire length of the canyon.

Regardless of what I write this true force of nature can in no way be relayed to you in print. The life force it has created here hosts dozens of endemic types of plants and flowers. The great limestone walls are home to eagles, falcons and hawks. The river has several types of trout and shellfish. The ridges are lined with tiny villages, ancestors of the last semi-nomadic shepherd tribes to roam these wild lands during Illyrian and Vlach tribal days – which long ago assimilated with newly arrived Slav tribes from the north. The ancient traditions and lifestyles are preserved more so by the power of geographical isolation than of human will.

There are forces here, especially within government, that are blind to the ecological value of the Rakitnica Canyon. They want to build roads and hydro-electric dams in one of the most pristine and untouched places in all of Europe. Bosnia and Herzegovina claims to strive towards European integration yet our environmental practices and amount of protected lands are amongst the worst in all of geographical Europe. The vast natural riches also attract European Union partners who willfully and knowingly support the exploitation of the country's water and forest resources. Unfortunately,

Bosnians seem to be more than willing to do business with the highest bidders – placing in jeopardy the lush forests and crystal clear rivers that are its greatest resource for a sustainable and healthy future. Hopefully the well-intended forces of science, logic and respect for nature will prevail in this saga – if not, Europe certainly loses one its most precious natural resources. The organization I work for, Green Visions, and several others, do organize trips to certain parts of the canyon in small, intimate groups – aimed at presenting to guests the richness of the cultural and natural heritage of the area.

I won't give you instructions on how to get there or what you can see and do. This place is a place of worship – and it should be treated as such. Leave no trace behind if you do go – and rest assured it will leave a lasting trace on you and your impressions of this stunningly beautiful country.

TO THE EAST

The eastern part of Bosnia is a very mountainous and isolated region. With the exception of **Goražde**, these far eastern ranges are largely populated by Bosnian Serbs. Few towns are industrialised and most depend on farming and shepherding for a living. The timber industry is rather significant as is the illegal exploitation of the region's forests.

One advantage of this so-called 'underdevelopment' is the large expanse of untouched wilderness and forests, and the tiny villages that still rely on the land for survival. The Drina Valley has a long cultural history and has been a crossroads of migration from Serbia, Sandžak and Montenegro. Many locals here share close ties with the people of these bordering regions. The Drina River has been a lifeline to the development and growth of this area, and from Foča to Višegrad many beautiful towns have been erected along her banks. The Drina is formed on the border of Montenegro where the Tara and Piva rivers meet. From this point the mighty Drina winds its way to Višegrad, where it heads north and forms the natural boundary between Bosnia and Serbia.

East Sarajevo (used to be Srpsko Sarajevo)

At times it's hard to tell if Srpsko Sarajevo is a city, a town or an entire region. Geographically speaking it only includes Pale to the east, and the suburbs of Lukavica and parts of Dobrinja to the south. Politically, however, East Sarajevo covers a much larger region including the towns of Rogatica, Sokolac, Srpska Ilidža, Srpski Stari Grad, Srpsko Novo Sarajevo (all those 'Srpski' names changed recently but are still widely used) and Trnovo.

When the Dayton Peace Accords were signed, the Bosnian Serbs left Sarajevo city in droves. Whether in fear of retaliation for the siege of Sarajevo, or under pressure from the Serbian nationalist parties (SDS and the Radical Party) to form a unified Serbian Sarajevo, a large portion of the original Serbian population of Sarajevo now live on the eastern outskirts of the city and call it Srpsko Sarajevo. The political and administrative centre for this large region is Pale.

Getting there and around

This is a difficult task. As East Sarajevo isn't really a place but more a region it is nearly impossible to give directions to and around it. The east

The Tara River has carved one of the world's deepest canyons on the border with Montenegro

In Sutjeska National Park the Skakavac waterfall flows from Perućica Forest, one of the last primeval forests in Europe

Whitewater rafting on the Tara River is one of the greatest adventures in the country

Trnovačko Lake in Sutjeska National Park, on the border with Montenegro

osnia and Herzegovina's highest peak - Mt. Maglić at 2,386 meters

The bridge on the River Drina in Višegrad

Stećci, the medieval tombstones of the Bosnian Church

road out of Sarajevo leads to Pale. This is the only road out of Sarajevo to the east, via Bentbaša near the old town. The first main junction is 12km east to the left and leads up Romanija Mountain to Sokolac, Rogatica and Prača. The road eventually meets up with the Drina Valley and connects with Goražde to the west and Višegrad to the east. Confused yet? If you carry straight on at the junction the road will take you to Pale, and from Pale there is only one mountain road to Jahorina Ski Centre.

To the southeast, near the airport, is the only other main route in East Sarajevo. This is the road that leads to Foča and travels through Trnovo and Dobro Polje. Near Foča the road again splits east and south. East leads to Goražde and south leads to Sutjeska National Park and eventually to Trebinje and Dubrovnik. Be aware that there are not many main routes in eastern Republika Srpska. The main arteries are all connected in a rather simple manner. It's just a matter of connecting the dots. A road map indicates all this quite clearly.

What to see and do

Romanija Mountain to the east dominates East Sarajevo. This lush, pine-covered mountain carries important historical significance for the Serbs. It is in these dense forests and scattered caves that Serbian hajduks (rebels) hid from the Ottoman armies. The most famous hiding spot is **Novak's Cave**. There is an excellent hiking trail to the cave with a wonderful view of Jahorina Mountain. The last 50m or so requires a bit of climbing but climbing gear is not necessary. The hajduks co-ordinated raids from their hide-outs in the heart of the mountain, and never gave in to Ottoman rule. Going even further back in time, on the **Glošina Plateau** between **Kopita and Romanija** mountains, are the remains of 2,000 gravestones believed to be dated before Christ. In the same area a large field of stećci mark the existence of the Bosnian Church (some claim it was the Orthodox Church or Bogumils).

There are many caves worth exploring in this region. The most significant archaeological finds were in the **Orlovača Caves**, which are perhaps the most fascinating of all the accessible caves in Bosnia. The remains of cave bears (Ursus spalaeus) found here are estimated to be more than 16,000 years old and one of the largest bear skulls found in Europe has been excavated here. The number, variety and size of the bones discovered make it one of the most significant palaeontological findings in the Balkans. There are professionally guided tours by students and professors from the University of Srpsko Sarajevo in Pale. The cave itself, located on the limestone massif of Orlovača Mountain, is estimated at over one and a half miles, and lit trails have been completed 700m deep into the cave. Digs in the vicinity of the cave suggest that a major prehistoric civilisation dating from the late Bronze Age flourished here. Even remnants from the early Neolithic age have been found in nearby caves. The entire area is ideal for picnics along the river that flows through the cave, or for a wander in the surrounding hills. The region is safe from mines. The entire area is now a base for scientific research and the funds raised from tourist visits are used to continue with excavations and educational activities. The cave and the excavation programme's email address is filozof@paleol.net. The students offer guided tours every day from 10.00 to 17.00 in the local language and English.

There are also caves in **Bogovići** and **Litovac**. **Lednjača Cave** is named after the ice that can be found inside even on a hot summer's day.

Orlovača Cave is the only cave that is marked and easily found. A guide is necessary for exploring the others.

The noble Pavlović family are said to have been the landlords of East Bosnia during Tvrtko Kotromanić's rule from 1353 to 1391. It is believed that the Pavlović's built the **Borac fortress** in 1415, on the Prača River near the present-day town of Rogatica. The **Prača River** is a tributary of the Drina and forms the long canyon between Rogatica and Goražde. The town of Rogatica doesn't offer much to the visitor, but **Borike Horse Farm** (tel: 058 410 925; fax: 058 415 332), 18km to the northeast and situated in the hills outside of Rogatica, is one of the most famous horse-raising farms for Bosnian mountain horses. There is a mountain lodge and restaurant on the premises. The restaurant serves traditional food and the accommodation is simple but nice. A single room with breakfast costs 40KM. It's one of the few places for jahanje, or horseback riding, in the country. One hour of riding costs 15KM without and 25KM with a guide. The open meadows for riding and the thick forests for walking make it a nice stop for those willing to wander through the back roads of east Bosnia. The **St Peter and Paul Apostles Church** in Borike, built in 1911, is an interesting place to soak in a bit of the religious heritage of the Serbs.

Other religious monuments worth seeing are the **St George Church** from 1886 in Trnovo, and **St Luke's Monastery** and church on **Mount Trebević**. The latter one is perhaps the most interesting church in the area. It is built in the old highland style with a wooden steeple and roof. Visitors are welcome and there are road signs off the main Trebević road to Jahorina from Sarajevo. Many of the churches in the region were built in the 1990s and although they are attractive they are not a historical representation of the old Orthodox churches of Bosnia and Herzegovina. Speaking of Mount Trebević, I highly recommend walkers to trek to the top of Trebević through the beautiful pine forest. The view of Sarajevo and the large panorama of mountains to the south are stunning. Trebević is mined in the parts closer to town. If you are travelling from town on Trebević towards Jahorina, the right side of the road is safe but, as always, I recommend a guide in any areas that can pose a threat.

The **Orthodox Ethno Gallery Ognjište** in Pale (Trifka Grabeza bb; tel: 057 225 779; fax: 057 224 622; email: ognjiste@paleol.net) not only exhibits Orthodox art and handicrafts, but is a gift shop with traditional musical instruments, pottery, clothes, literature and music.

Treskavica Mountain

Treskavica changed hands half a dozen times during the war and is therefore densely mined. However, it is remembered as the most beautiful mountain in the region, especially its four glacier lakes and dozens of smaller mountain lakes. It is said that there are more than 300 water sources throughout the entire range. Its highest peak, **Paklješ** or Ćaba Peak (Ćaba means mecca from the Arabic word 'Kaba') at 2,086m, is one of the most remarkable tooth-shaped peaks in the country. Hikers and mountaineers do travel on Treskavica but do not explore it on your own. If you must see it, like I did, then find an experienced guide who knows the mountain well. Stick to the trails. There are so many other beautiful mountains in the country and, at least until this mountain is thoroughly de-mined, it is probably wisest to skip it.

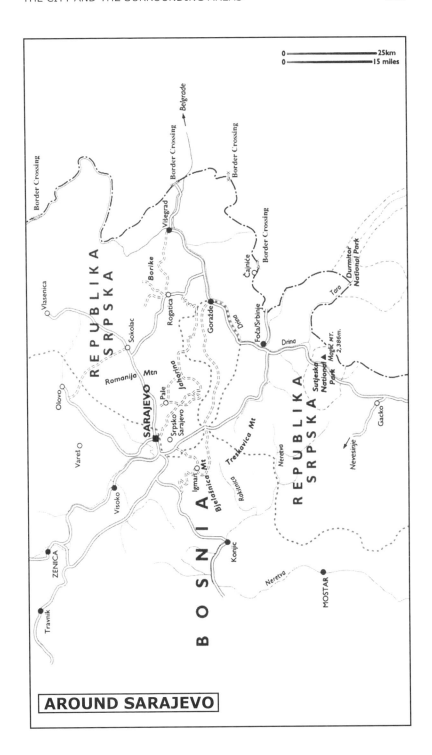

AROUND SARAJEVO

Sutjeska National Park

Sutjeska is one of Bosnia and Herzegovina's oldest parks. It is famous for the Partisan victory over the Germans in WWII and there are large stone monuments commemorating the event. The park itself is 17,500 hectares of magnificent and untouched wilderness. It hosts one of the last two remaining primeval forests in Europe, called Perućica. Beech trees tower over 60 metres high and endemic black pines stem from the rocky faces that protect the ancient forest. Skakavac waterfall can be seen from the look-out point – this two hundred feet plus waterfall is dwarfed by the massive blanket of green trees that cover the valley.

The Sutjeska River has carved a stunning valley through the middle of the park and divides Zelengora (Green Peaks) Mountain from Maglić and Volujak Mountains. Bosnia and Herzegovina's highest peak, Maglić at over 2,386m, is located in the park, directly on the border with Montenegro. It presents a challenging climb for even experienced hikers. The park has a hotel in Tjentište (the flat valley along the River Sutjeska) and a café and restaurant. The hotel is socialist style and not particularly attractive but the nature within the park border competes with that found anywhere in Europe. Zelengora Mountain is great for hiking and walking and there are several newly renovated mountain huts on the mountain. Bear and wolf sightings are common. The park, although maintaining its pristine nature, is not well organized in terms of marked paths, good maps, or visitor information.

Before entering the park, you need to buy a 1.50KM costing ticket from the hotel reception of, if staffed, at one of the park entrances. Access to Perućica, the primeval forest, requires the company of one of the park guides, none of which speaks English. A park guide costs 50KM for a day and can be arranged by phone (058 520 112 - no English spoken).

Getting there and around

Travelling from Sarajevo, take the Sarajevo-Trnovo road almost to Foča before turning right (roads are marked) for the Trebinje-Dubrovnik road. Once you turn right expect the road to become a bit narrower as you climb, the curvy bends barely giving you enough room to stay on your side of the solid line. Once you reach the top of the mountain (you'll know when you're there!) the massive faces of Zelengora and Maglić dominate the view. It's all downhill from there. Beware of the unconcerned cows on the road. After the petrol station (which seems like it is always closed) you'll be in Tjentište. This is where **Hotel Mladost** (tel: 058 572 556/520 118 - they rarely pick up), a restaurant and maybe even some information can be found.

At **Tjentište** you'll find an enormous monument built in remembrance of the **Battle of Sutjeska**. The sheer enormity of it makes it worth a look. From Tjentište you will need approximately 30 minutes to reach the scenic view area of **Perućica primeval forest**. Unfortunately the signs are in Cyrillic. But once you've driven for some time on gravel road the first piece of asphalt that you reach will be the Perućica stop. The walk out to the ridge is only about ten minutes and it is an utterly amazing view. Bring a camera. The second stop is only 100m away at **Dragoš Sedlo**. This sign is also in Cyrillic. Off to the left is a small hill, literally 20m away. From that spot you get a magnificent view of **Maglić Mountain**, the highest point in Bosnia and Herzegovina at 2,386m above sea level. Down to the right of the road is a natural water fountain of potable water (trust me) and the beginning of the marked trails that lead through Perućica. The trails are marked but these are not always easily visible. They lead deep into the last primeval forest in Europe. It's not a hard hike but you should be wearing good shoes and if you're not in the best of shape maybe it would be better to drive up to the next spot, **Prijevor.**

From Dragoš Sedlo you'll travel another 4-5km before coming to a right turn. It's the first and only turn-off and the one you want to take. Another 3-4km on and you'll reach Prijevor at 1,668m. Park here. The long, bald ridge in front of you is great for a picnic, stroll or a good hour-long walk. Following the road you came in on will lead you to **Trnovačko Lake** (we're on foot now). The trail is obvious for most of the way and then you'll have to use your trekking senses if you'd like to make it all the way to the lake. Bring your passports with you; you have just crossed into **Montenegro**. There may be a park ranger who will check your passports.

Back at Tjentište, if you'd like to travel to the other side of the park to **Zelengora** (green heights) **Mountain** then you should turn left out of the hotel car park and left again after the petrol station. The drive to **Donje Bare** is only 15km to the northeast but it will take a good hour to get there. The road is gravel and you will climb 1,000m before you reach the six-man mountain hut. There is usually a ranger at the hut but here you are free to roam wherever you like. Open meadows and beech-tree forests surround this tranquil lake. Walking further on you stand the chance of spotting a bear. Wolves roam the area but sightings are rare.

If you travel south on the main road (past the cows) towards **Gacko-Trebinje-Dubrovnik** you'll enter the rugged canyon of the river after which the park is named. The Sutjeska River has carved out this deep canyon lined with endemic Munika black pines. There are several places along the river to stop for a picnic or to simply stand in awe.

Tara River

Getting there

The Tara River runs along the border with Montenegro and is best approached from Foča and with a guide. The small dirt tracks along the Tara on the Bosnian side are not clearly marked and it is easy to get lost. The easiest approach is from the Durmitor Park in Montenegro but that requires border crossings and more directions. Stick with the guide when searching out the Tara River. Foča is accessible from the south via Trebinje-Gacko-Sutjeska National Park if you are coming from the coast or Herzegovina. From Sarajevo, the main southeast route via Trnovo and Dobro Polje leads directly to Foča.

What to see and do

Coined the 'jewel of Europe' (by the locals of course), this wild, turquoise blue river is a raging mass of water fed by the towering mountains of **Durmitor National Park** in Montenegro. The Tara River traverses along the border of Bosnia and Montenegro, with 30km of it in Bosnia and the rest belonging to the other side. It rises from the mountain ranges in the northern part of Montenegro and flows 140km until meeting with the **Piva River** and forming the **River Drina**, one of the longest and largest rivers in the Balkans.

For eons the powerful flow of the Tara River has hollowed out a soft limestone surface, creating the sculpted form of gorges and chasms that we see today. Age-old earth erosion has created the 82km-long canyon, the second largest canyon in the world after Colorado. At its deepest the canyon soars 1,300m high. In a few places the Tara gives the impression that its furious flow is beginning to calm, but it always gathers momentum and continues its dramatic flow to the Drina.

Along the river banks the vegetation is very dense: black pine, eastern hornbeam, black ash, elm, linden and in higher areas one can see cork oaks, hornbeams, maples and beech trees. In the areas above the 1,000m mark there are fir and spruce forests. The black pine forests are of special interest. Crni pod, or the black floor, is home to unusually high trees. Some stretch as high as 50m and are over 400 years old.

Aside from nature lovers and fishermen, the river attracts a large number of adrenaline junkies. Rated at level 3-5, it offers some of the most intense and challenging rafting in Europe. A ride on one of the 'real' rafts, logs tied together and guided by a massive wooden rudder, is quite an experience. There are, of course, rafting outfits that provide sturdy and safe rubber rafts with all the necessary gear. Most groups operate out of Foča (there are also several rafting agencies in Montenegro) and offer breakfast, lunch and overnight camping in their rafting packages. The caving association **Ursus Spelaeus** (tel: 058 210 656/065 528 721) from Foča organises trips as well as Green Visions and Rafting Tours from Sarajevo (see Sarajevo Tour Operators).

Foča

In the eyes of the international community this town has got one of the worst reputations in the country for its hard-line nationalist politics. It is said that war criminals are harboured here and the return of minority groups (mainly Muslims) is proceeding slowly.

There is some truth to Foča's reputation (now called Srbinje by the Serbs). During World War II the Bosnian Muslim population was slaughtered and it is said that the Drina ran red with blood. There are similar stories told about the last war. Having said that, it always strikes me that most of the town folk, as a matter of fact, are quite friendly (provided you avoid a history discussion), and for the casual visitor Foča is quite a nice little town. It lies on the edge of the mighty Drina River only 75km southeast of Sarajevo.

The **Ćehotina River** flows through the town and feeds the Drina. The surrounding mountains are wild and beautiful. Hunting and fishing are popular sports in this region. Fly fishing there is amongst the best in the country. Wildlife is teeming in the dense forest towards the border with Montenegro. Foča is also the gathering point for rafting on the Tara.

There is accommodation in town at the **Motel Brioni** (tel: 058 210 646) on the Ćehotina River, and two good restaurants, **Drina** (tel: 058 214 470) and **Aleksandrija** (tel: 058 575 544) on the Drina River. For hunting contact the **Hunting Association of Republika Srpska** (tel: 057 447 052; email: lsrs@paleol.net).

Goražde

Goražde is the largest east Bosnian town in the **Drina Valley**. It has long been a thriving stopover along the trading routes from Serbia and Montenegro to Sarajevo, but many foreigners know Goražde only as the last UN safe zone not to fall to the Bosnian Serb offensives that had overrun **Srebrenica** and **Žepa.** This enclave was completely cut off from the rest of Bosnian government-controlled territory and was heavily bombed during the three-year siege. You can still see the anti-sniper bridge that was built underneath the central pedestrian bridge to provide safe passage from one side to the other.

Today's Goražde has changed considerably and is quite a bit brighter. The Drina is a favourite spot for swimming and rafting and the café's and restaurants along its banks are always full. To the south of Goražde is one of the largest medieval graveyards in the country. It is estimated that around 600 stećci are in one hillside cemetery. Some of the old mahalas from Ottoman times remain in decent condition, and there are still a few old-style homes in the centre of town. The mosques have been restored and the call to prayer can again be heard echoing through the valley. Alongside its Islamic culture, Goražde has a significant Orthodox history, as is evident from the Orthodox church here, built in 1446. Less than a century later, in 1521, this church owned the country's first printing press.

Every August, Goražde hosts the wonderful International Friendship Festival. The town fills up with artists performing and giving workshops to both adults and children. For most people in Goražde this is the most important cultural event of the year. It started off as a four-day event in 1997, but had spread to a full ten days by 2004.

Višegrad

This town, too, has seen better days. Višegrad is a strikingly beautiful settlement along the Drina River, almost on the border with Serbia. The town is famous for the **Ćuprija na Drini** (Bridge on the Drina) which is a magnificent Ottoman structure spanning the wide river. It gained its fame from the Nobel Prize for Literature winner Ivo Andrić and his novel Bridge on the Drina. The old part of town, once a charming example of old Ottoman architecture, is in dire need of maintenance. The area around Višegrad, however, is wild and untamed. In the remote hills towards the border one can hear the howl of wolves at night. **Dobrun Monastery**, built in 1343, is one of the oldest monasteries in the country. It is open to visitors but you may have trouble finding it if you're not with a guide.

To the west the deep gorge of the **Lim River** plunges into the Drina from **Rudo.** The Lim originates in the Prokletija Mountains (the end of the Dinaric chain) in the small Montenegrin town of Plav. Hunting is quite a popular sport and the Drina always seems willing to sacrifice some of her biggest fish to anglers. There are no organised tourist activities or even a sign to tell you where you are. You can visit the **Gradska galerija** (town gallery) at Užičkog korpusa 14 and the **People's Library Ivo Andrić** on the same street. For the wandering soul it's an interesting place to sit on the bridge and soak up the energy of the Drina racing below you. The villagers may look at you with a bit of suspicion at first but after the first rakija you'll have made a few new friends.

The Ecotourism Experience, *by John Snyder*

There are few cities in the world that can offer such magnificent eco-tourism opportunities so close to the capital. Sarajevo's geographic location lends itself to the wild terrain of the central Dinaric Alps stretching deep into Herzegovina and east to Sutjeska National Park. From easy day walks and recreation areas to great skiing, whitewater adventures and magnificent hiking, biking, wildlife viewing and caving - there is a plethora of pristine areas to visit while staying in Sarajevo or visiting the eastern border region with Serbia and Montenegro.

Green Visions

As Bosnia and Herzegovina's leading eco-tourism and environmental group, this group of young professionals have pioneered the responsible and sustainable tourism movement in Bosnia and Herzegovina. They are dedicated to promoting and preserving the cultural and natural heritage of the highland areas and strictly honour environmental codes of 'leave no trace.' Based out of Sarajevo they offer hikes, walks, biking, rafting, tour skiing and a wonderfully unique opportunity to experience the old world highland traditions in the many villages that still survive in the high mountain regions. They offer one-day trips during most of the year but also a great range of five to ten day tours that lead you to the most remote and beautiful areas in the country.

One can immediately see the strong relations Green Visions has with the villagers and the nature they are so dependent on. An outing with them will not only give you an authentic wilderness experience but also support environmental activities and the villages you are visiting. They speak Bosnian, English, French and Dutch. Contact info: Green Visions, Radnička bb; tel/fax: +387 33 717 290/291; e-mail: sarajevo@greenvisions.ba; web: www.greenvisions.ba.

WILDLIFE VIEWING: BIRDING AND PHOTO SAFARIS

The Ecotourism Experience

Wildlife viewing in the midst of the forest is the single greatest attraction to ecotourists. This is the place to do it. This region's diversity and abundance of wildlife species, and the opportunities it offers to see rare and endangered mammals and birds, make a visit to this area an eco-tourism experience that is unique in the world.

Photo safari guide services are provided by the hunting clubs in the communities around Sarajevo, Foča and Goražde as well as by Green Visions. The members of these organizations have many years of experience and profound knowledge of the forests and wildlife in the entire Sarajevo and Sutjeska region. They don't just speak about the wildlife you come across, but also explain

The unique traditional attire of the Bjelašnica highlanders can still be found today in many of the isolated mountain villages

Lukomir village on Bjelašnica Mountain is the highest and most isolated village in the country

The older generation carries on the tradition of handmade dress

The hidden waterfall of Lučica near Mt. Bukovik is only 5 kilometers from the center of Sarajevo

the environmental conditions that enable the animals to survive.

In line with the eco-philosophy of maximizing enjoyment and mini-mizing disruption, guides limit the size of their groups. Depend-ing on where you're going you may hike all the way from town, travel a bit by car, or move into the forests with off-road vehicles. Either way, you are likely to be provided with an introduction to the wildlife prior to your departure.

GUIDELINES FOR PHOTO SAFARIS

The elimination of human profiles and smells is very important. Don't stand against a skyline. Wear clothing that blends with your environment. Do not act like a predator. Crawl, don't walk when approaching wildlife from short distances. Move in oblique or zig-zag patterns and exercise extreme patience. Adapt yourself to circumstances and be aware of how the animals respect your presence. If you respect their needs and desires, they will often accept you.

Stalking (tracking) is the most commonly used method for ap-proaching wild animals to get a good photograph. Binoculars and spotting scopes are helpful in locating animals at a distance. Be sure to scan the entire area to determine if there is more than one animal in the vicinity. For example, the safe way to photo-graph a bear is to be certain that there are no cubs in the area. Before stringing off for your animal, have your camera ready to go and mounted on the tripod. Anticipate where the animal will be when you get close enough to get a good picture. Plan your approach to the animal so that lighting and background will pro-duce the best possible picture.

When you get close to an animal and it is aware of you, be pa-tient. Allow the animal to adjust to your presence. Move only when it is busy feeding or otherwise occupied in an activity that will make it less likely to notice your movement. Once you are in its view, it is best to remain in the open where your subject can keep track of you. Never block an animal's escape path.

Take your pictures as discreetly as possible in order to get more natural poses and cause the animal the least distress. Ideally, you should stalk, photograph, and leave without unreasonably disturbing the animal. When you achieve this, you are an excel-lent stalker and ethical photographer.

A good understanding of the animal's behavior is helpful when stalking. Some species that live in open habitats, such as bear and wolves, may approach rather than flee from you once they spotted you. They come closer to catch your scent before decid-ing to escape. This behavior often provides an ideal opportunity for photographs.

Special care should be taken around nests and dens where dis-turbance can lead to abandonment and death of eggs and young. Extreme caution should be used when photographing young ani-mals – the mother is around somewhere and will be very protective. Always consider the consequence of your photographic activities on both the animal's and your own well-being.

SAFETY

Snakes: There are two species of poisonous snakes in Bosnia and Herzegovina. One of them is a viper and the other one is an adder. Both are hemeotoxic (blood poisoning) and bites require immediate medical attention. A bite wound will display swelling and skin discoloration.

Bears: Confrontations with the European brown bear (*Ursus arctos*) are rare. If you do encounter this type of bear: do not run as this will trigger the bear's predator instincts and it will quickly pursue and overtake you. Instead, back away slowly. If an attack is imminent lay on the ground and curl into a ball covering your head and neck with your arms. Never approach bear cubs as the mother will be nearby and is likely to attack you.

Wolves: The wolf (*Cannis lupus*) roams freely throughout this region. They will avoid humans. If you see wolves then attempt to stay upwind of their position. Allow them to migrate through your area.

Wild Boar: These animals also roam freely through the region. Because these animals are hunted they fear man. However, wild boar are belligerent by nature and are especially dangerous when protecting their young.

Wildlife Species

Perhaps the most remarkable environmental characteristic of Sarajevo is that it is the home of complete range of environmental systems. All of the animals that are essential for sustaining the region's ecology are present. This means that animals ranging from dominant predators to very small wildlife species may be found in this region. These conditions and the presence of these animals provide a potentially valuable opportunity for the tourist to view wildlife in their natural habitats. Sutjeska National Park is perhaps the best region in the country for wildlife viewing. The vast wilderness here stretches deep into Montenegro's western border and is teeming with wildlife of all sorts.

A representative list of the wildlife species in the Sarajevo region, particularly to the east in Republika Srpska includes the following:

- European brown bear (*Ursus arctos*)
- Wolves (*Canis lupus*)
- Chamois (*Rupicapra rupicapra*)
- Roe deer (*Capreolus capreolus*)
- Wild boar (*Sus scrofa*)
- Wild cat (*Felis silvestris*)

- Marten (*Martes foina*)
- Badger (*Meles meles*)
- Foxes (*Vulpes vulpes*)
- Rabbit (*Lepus europaeus*)
- Squirrel (*Sciursus vulgaris*)

SPORTFISHING

The plethora of crystal clear river and lake systems in eastern Bosnia has a remarkable diversity of trophy sport fish species. First class river fishing is possible on the Drina River. Other rivers offering great fishing opportunities are Lim near Rudo and the Tara and Ćehotina near Foča. The name for each species of fish described below is provided in English, Bosnian/Croatian/Serbian, and in the Latin biological name.

- **Grayling – Lipen** (*Thymallus thymalus*)

  Flies for Grayling

Adams Dry	Mosquito Larva
Elk Wing Caddis	Pheasant Tail Nymph
Gold Ribbed Hare's Ear	Salmon Fry
Humpy	Tellico
Mosquito Dry	Zug Bug
Light Cahill	Black Gnat
Polar Shrimp	Orange Woolly Bugger

- **California Trout - Kalifornijska pastrmka** (*Salmo iridens*)

  Flies for California Trout

Adams Dry	Iliama Pinkie
Bunny Fly	Mirabou Muddler
Egg Sucking Leech	Pheasant Tail Nymph
Elk Wing Caddis	Polar Shrimp
Gold Ribbed Hare's Ear	Woolly Bugger

- **Brook Trout - Amerikanski somic cvergi** (*Amirus nebulosus*)

  Flies for Brook Trout

Baby Needlefish	Iliama Pinkie
Blue Smolt	Muddler Minnow
Gastineau Smolt	Pheasant Tail Nymph
Gold Ribbed Hare's Ear	Roselyn's Sand Lance
Humpy	Woolly Bugger

HERB AND MUSHROOM COLLECTION

The forests, fields, and river valleys around Sarajevo and in eastern Bosnia contain a diversity of herbs and mushrooms that have many useful purposes. The people of this region use their many natural resources for food, medicines, and fragrances. They also obtain income from the sale of herbs and mushrooms.

Given the distinct environmental characteristics found in each of the region's communities, there is a remarkable diversity of herbs and mushrooms available for collection. Eastern Bosnia can provide the tourist with very different herb and mushroom collection experiences. The highlands offer the outdoor experiences of a mountain valley. The Dinaric Alps provide the natural setting for plants that are uniquely adapted to high mountain environments. The herb and mushroom collection tourism experience is both an enjoyable gathering activity and a rewarding way to learn about the region's natural environment.

The highland regions have numerous species of herbs and mushrooms, but are particularly well known for its fruits and berries. The growing conditions in this area are well suited for the growing of plums, apples, pear, sour cherries, currant, raspberry, and strawberry. The entire region around Sarajevo frequently enjoys a large harvest of these fruits and berries and they ship part of this harvest to food processing plants. They also make local fruit products. Home production includes juices, jams, and a very high quality brandy.

Types of Herbs and Mushrooms and Collection Calendar

Forest Products	Collecting Calendar
Wild cherry	June
Wild pear	September – October
Wild apple	October
Cornel	October
Sloe, blackberry	September – October
Hazelnut	October
Bilberry	October

Mushrooms	Collecting Calendar
Boletus mushrooms	
Yellow chanterelle	
Button mushroom	Summer-autumn

Medicinal Herbs	Collecting Calendar
Linden flower	
Elder flower	
Hawthorn flower	
Blackberry flower	
Klamath flower	

Vervain flower   May, June and July
Black thorn flower
Meadow saffron flower
Camomile flower
Mint flower

Medicinal Herbs   **Collecting Calendar**
Hawthorn
Dog rose
Mountain pine
Bilberry
Plod mukinje   September - October
Raspberry
Blackberry
Thorns
Strawberry

Medicinal Herbs   **Collecting Calendar**
Gentian root
Wild tobacco root   September and October
Herbs
Sallow
Horse - tail
Wild thyme   From June to September
Hernia
Sweet fern
Nettle

APPENDIX: LANGUAGE

Pronunciation

Latin	Cyrillic	
A, a	А, а	as in party
B, b	Б, б	as in bed
C, c	Ц, ц	as in fats, bats
Č, č	Ч, ч	as in culture
Ć, ć	Ћ, ћ	as in cheese
D, d	Д, д	as in doctor
Dž, dž	Џ, џ	as in jam
Đ, đ	Ђ, ђ	as in jazz
E, e	Е, е	as in pet
F, f	Ф, ф	as in free
G, g	Г, г	as in goat
H, h	Х, х	as in hat
I, i	И, и	as in feet
J, j	Ј, ј	as in yet
K, k	К, к	as in kept
L, l	Л, л	as in leg
Lj, lj	Љ, љ	
M, m	М, м	as in mother
N, n	Н, н	as in no
Nj, nj	Њ, њ	as in new
O, o	О, о	as in hot
P, p	П, п	as in pie
R, r	Р, р	as in air
S, s	С, с	as in sand
Š, š	Ш, ш	as in shovel
T, t	Т, т	as in too
U, u	У, у	as in look
V, v	В, в	as in very
Z, z	З, з	as in zoo
Ž, ž	Ж, ж	as in treasure

Greetings

Good morning	*Dobro jutro*	Good afternoon	*Dobar dan*
Good evening	*Dobro veče* [dobro veche]		
Good night	*Laku noć*	Hello/Goodbye	*Ćao* [chao]
What is your name?	*Kako se zoveš?*	How are you?	*Kako si?*
I am well	*Dobro sam*		

Basic phrases

please	*molim Vas*	thank you	*hvala*
you're welcome	*nema na čemu* (reply to thank you)		
there is no	*nema*	excuse me	*oprostite*
give me	*dajte mi*	I like to	*želim*
I would like	*volio bih*	how?	*kako?*
how much?	*koliko?*	how much (cost)?	*koliko košta?*
what?	*šta?*	what's this ?	*šta je ovo?*
who?	*ko?*	when?	*kada?*
where?	*gdje?*	from where?	*odakle?*
where is	*gdje je*	do you know?	*znate li?*
I don't know	*ne znam*	I don't understand	*ne razumijem*
yes	*da*	no	*ne*
perhaps	*možda*	good	*dobro/dobra* (m/f)
how do you say?	*kako se kaže?*		

Numbers

one	*jedan*	nine	*devet*
two	*dva*	ten	*deset*
three	*tri*	eleven	*jedanaest*
four	*četiri*	sixteen	*šesnaest*
five	*pet*	twenty	*dvadeset*
six	*šest*	thirty one	*trideset i jedan*
seven	*sedam*	one hundred	*stotina*
eight	*osam*	one thousand	*hiljada/tisuća*

Food and drink

baked	*pečeno*	beef	*govedina*
beer	*pivo*	boiled	*kuhano*
bon appetite	*prijatno*	brandy	*loza*
bread	*hljeb/kruh*	breakfast	*doručak* [doruchak]
cabbage	*kupus*	cake	*kolač*
cheese	*sir*	coffee	*kafa/kava/kahva*
cucumber	*krastavac*	bean	*grah*
chicken	*piletina*	chips, french fries	*pomfrit*
dinner	*večera*	drink (noun)	*piće*
drink (verb)	*piti*	eggs	*jaja*
fish	*riba*	fried	*prženo*
fruit	*voće*	grilled	*sa roštilja*
home-made	*domaće*	juice	*đus*
lamb	*janjetina*	lemon	*limun*

lunch	*ručak*	meat	*meso*
milk	*mlijeko*	onion	*luk*
orange	*naranča*	pasta	*makaroni*
pears	*kruške*	peaches	*breskve*
plums	*šljive*	pork	*svinjetina*
potato	*krompir*	restaurant	*restoran*
rice	*riža*	salt	*so*
soup	*supa*	spirit	*rakija*
sugar	*šećer*	tomato	*paradajz*
tea	*čaj*	to eat	*jesti*
veal	*teletina*	vegetables	*povrće*
water	*voda*	wine	*vino*

Shopping

bank	*banka*	money	*novac*
bookshop	*knjižara*	postcard	*razglednica*
chemist	*apoteka*	post office	*pošta*
market	*pijaca*	shop	*prodavnica*

Getting around

bus	*autobus*	left/right	*lijevo/desno*
bus station	*autobusna stanica (autobusni kolodvor)*	straight on	*pravo*
train station	*željeznička stanica (željeznički kolodvor)*	ahead/behind	*naprijed/iza*
plane/airport	*avion/aerodrom (avion/zračna luka)*	up/down	*gore/dolje*
car/taxi	*auto/taxi*	under/over	*ispod/iznad*
petrol	*benzin*	north/south	*sjever/jug*
petrol station	*benzinska pumpa*	east/west	*istok/zapad*
entrance/exit	*ulaz/izlaz*	road/bridge	*put/most*
arrival/departure	*dolazak/polazak*	hill/mountain	*brdo/planina*
open/closed	*otvoreno/zatvoreno*	village/town	*selo/grad*
here/there	*ovdje/tamo*	waterfall	*vodopad*
near/far	*blizu/daleko*		

Time

hour/minute	*sat/minuta*	today/tomorrow	*danas/sutra*
week/day	*sedmica/dan (tjedan/dan)*	yesterday	*jučer*
year/month	*godlna/mjesec*	morning	*jutro*
now	*sada*	afternoon	*poslijepodne*
soon	*uskoro*	evening/night	*večer/noć*
Monday	*ponedjeljak*	Friday	*petak*
Tuesday	*utorak*	Saturday	*subota*
Wednesday	*srijeda*	Sunday	*nedjelja*
Thursday	*četvrtak*	spring	*proljeće*
autumn	*jesen*	summer	*ljeto*
winter	*zima*		

Other useful words

a little	*malo*	a lot	*puno*
after	*poslije*	bathroom	*kupatilo*
bed	*krevet*	before	*prije*
block (of buildings)	*zgrade*	book	*knjiga*
car	*auto*	child	*dijete*
church	*crkva*	city	*grad*
cold	*hladno*	currency	*valuta*
dentist	*zubar*	doctor	*doktor*
dry	*suho*	embassy	*ambasada*
enough	*dosta*	fever	*temperatura*
film	*film*	hill	*brdo*
hospital	*bolnica*	hot	*toplo*
hotel	*hotel*	house	*kuća*
hut	*koliba*	ill	*bolestan*
key	*ključ*	lake	*jezero*
large	*veliko*	lorry	*kamion*
mosque	*džamija*	never	*nikad*
night	*noć*	nightclub	*disko*
nothing	*ništa*	police	*policija*
railway	*željeznica*	rain	*kiša*
river	*rijeka*	road	*put*
room	*soba*	sea	*more*
small	*malo*	street	*ulica*
to hurt	*boljeti*	to swim	*plivati*
toilet paper	*toalet papir*	too much	*previše*
tourist office	*turistički ured*	train	*voz/vlak*
village	*selo*	you	*Vi/ ti*

APPENDIX:
MORE INFORMATION

BOOKS

History/Politics

Simms, Brendan *Unfinest Hour; How Britain Helped to Destroy Bosnia* Penguin Press 2003

Malcolm, Noel *Bosnia, A short history* London Macmillan1994

Maas, Peter *Love Thy Neighbour* Papermac 1996

Lovrenović, Ivan *Bosnia, A Cultural History* Saqi Books 2001

Glenny, Misha *The Balkans 1804-1999, Nationalism, War and the Great Powers* Granta Books 2000 (second edition)

Holbrooke, Richard *To end a war* Modern Library 1998

Gutman, Roy *Witness to Genocide* Element Books 1993

Literature from Bosnia and Herzegovina (published in English)

Jergović, Miljenko *Sarajevo Marlboro* Consortium Book 2004

Selimović, Meša *Death of the Dervish* Northwestern University Press 1996

Andrić, Ivo *Bridge over the Drina* Harvill Press 1995

Hemon, Aleksandar *Question of Bruno* Picador 2001

Hemon, Aleksandar *Nowhere man* Picador 2003

WEBSITES

The web is being used more and more in Bosnia and Herzegovina these days. It is not, however, used on the scale as in the west. Most sites are, logically, in the local language, but there are quite a few good and helpful websites in English as well. Some of them simply offer a different angle as to what is going on in the country. When checking these sites you'll find some better than others but they all have some value for those looking to get to know Bosnia and Herzegovina a little bit better.

General

www.bosnia.org.uk - is the Bosnian Institute site that is a tremendous source of inside info and links to many local sites.

www.unsa.ba – University of Sarajevo gives a little insight as to what programs are available, what people are learning and what students in this part of the world are all about.

www.sarajevo-airport.ba – Flight schedules and other miscellaneous information about the coming and going to Sarajevo are available on this site.

www.imenik.telecom.ba – Online phone directory

www.rtvbih.ba – This is the official site of the Bosnia and Herzegovina National TV.

www.bhmac.org - is the official site of the Mine Action Center. It's not to scare you, it's meant to inform you.

Government

www.mvp.gov.ba – the Ministry of Foreign Affairs site gives an general overview of visa requirements and embassies here and abroad.

www.komorabih.com – this is the website of the Chambers of Foreign Commerce. The info provided is good and has many links to other informative sites in the country.

www.britishcouncil.ba - the British Council supports many cultural and educational activities. They are very up to date on the culture scene in BiH.

www.usis.com.ba – The American Embassy in BiH is very active. The site will give American citizens all the information they need while traveling as an American here.

www.ohr.int – The Office of the High Representative in BiH is the international governing body in the country. There are many updates on the economy, human rights, reform, and general info about who is who and what's going on in Bosnia and Herzegovina.

Tourism

www.bhtourism.ba – We made this site back in 2002. It's an OK site, but won't provide you with any information that is not already in this guide book series. There are plans to expand this site in the course of 2005.

www.sarajevo-tourism.com – Tourism Association of Sarajevo Canton is good site for general tourist information.

www.touristguide-ba.com – is a yellow pages 'tour guide' for the country. It does list an incredible amount of hotels, banks, restaurants, and even car repair garages. It may be of some help if you're looking for something in particular but the organization of it is not totally coherent.

www.sarajevo.ba - a site on the city of Sarajevo, what there is to see and what's happening in the fastest changing city in Europe.

www.city.ba - current events on cultural events in Sarajevo.

www.hercegovina.ba - a comprehensive web site on tourism in Herzegovina.

www.greenvisions.ba - an informative site on general information, eco-tourism, the environment and community development projects.

www.plivatourism.ba - an excellent site on eco-tourism in the Jajce area of central Bosnia.

www.veleztourism.ba - this site covers the cultural and natural heritage of the Blagaj and Mt. Velež area south of Mostar, including activities and accommodation.

Other interesting websites

Country history	http://vlib.iue.it/history/europe/Bosnia/
Country history	http://en.wikipedia.org/wiki/History of Bosnia and Herzegovina
Country history	http://www.kakarigi.net/manu/briefhis.htm
Historical maps	http://www.nytimes.com/specials/bosnia/context/ yugo1815.GIF.html
War history	http://www.friendsofbosnia.org/edu_bos.html
Towns and cities	http://www.fallingrain.com/world/BK/
Sarajevo	http://uvod.sarajevo.ba/
Banja Luka	http://www.banjaluka.rs.ba/_e/default.aspx
Mostar	http://en.wikipedia.org/wiki/Mostar
Tuzla	http://www.hr/tuzla/
Bihać	http://www.bihac.org/fotos/indexeng.html
Tourist guide	http://www.bosnie-herzegovina.net/e frames.html?/e toe.html
General info	http://www.bosnia-herzegowina.starttips.com/
Government	http://www.fbihvlada.gov.ba/#
Federation Gov.	http://www.fbihvlada.gov.ba/engleski/index.html
Rep. Srpska Gov.	http://www.vladars.net/en/
Canton Sarajevo	http://www.ks.gov.ba/eng/index.htm
Politics	http://en.wikipedia.org/wiki/Politics of Bosnia and Herzegovina

INDEX